WITHDRAWN

SAFETY

Classroom Safety Tips:

- Read all steps before you start.

- Listen to the teacher.

- When you see this , it means for you to be careful.

-  Wear goggles or gloves when told.

- Wear old clothes.

- Be careful with glass and sharp objects.

- Never taste or smell things unless your teacher tells you to.

- Clean up spills right away.

- Report accidents right away.

- Keep your work place neat.

- Clean up when you are done.

Outside Safety Tips:

- Listen to the teacher.

- Stay with your group.

- Never taste or smell things unless your teacher tells you to.

- Don't touch plants or animals unless your teacher tells you to.

- Put living things back where you found them.

- Report accidents right away.

REFERENCE--NOT TO BE TAKEN FROM THIS ROOM

ROCHESTER COLLEGE
MUIRHEAD LIBRARY
800 WEST AVON ROAD
ROCHESTER HILLS MI 48307

D1401275

EDU
Q
161.2
.M34
2000
v. 2

McGRAW-HILL
SCIENCE

MACMILLAN/McGRAW-HILL EDITION

RICHARD MOYER ■ LUCY DANIEL ■ JAY HACKETT

PRENTICE BAPTISTE ■ PAMELA STRYKER ■ JOANNE VASQUEZ

NATIONAL
GEOGRAPHIC
SOCIETY

McGraw-Hill
School Division

New York   Farmington

PROGRAM AUTHORS

Lucy H. Daniel, Ed.D.
*Teacher, Consultant
Rutherford County Schools,
North Carolina*

Dr. Jay Hackett
*Emeritus Professor of Earth
Sciences
University of Northern
Colorado*

Dr. Richard H. Moyer
*Professor of Science
Education
University of Michigan-
Dearborn*

Dr. H. Prentice Baptiste
*Professor of Curriculum and
Instruction
New Mexico State
University*

Pamela Stryker, M.Ed.
*Elementary Educator and
Science Consultant
Eanes Independent School
District
Austin, Texas*

JoAnne Vasquez
*Elementary Science
Education Specialist
Mesa Public Schools,
Arizona
NSTA President 1996–1997*

NATIONAL
GEOGRAPHIC
SOCIETY

Washington, D.C.

CONTRIBUTING AUTHORS
Dr. Thomas Custer
Dr. James Flood
Dr. Diane Lapp
Doug Llewellyn
Dorothy Reid
Dr. Donald M. Silver

CONSULTANTS
Dr. Danny J. Ballard
Dr. Carol Baskin
Dr. Bonnie Buratti
Dr. Suellen Cabe
Dr. Shawn Carlson
Dr. Thomas A. Davies
Dr. Marie DiBerardino
Dr. R. E. Duhrkopf
Dr. Ed Geary
Dr. Susan C. Giarratano-Russell
Dr. Karen Kwitter
Dr. Donna Lloyd-Kolkin
Ericka Lochner, RN
Dr. Dennis L. Nelson
Dr. Fred S. Sack
Dr. Martin VanDyke
Dr. E. Peter Volpe
Dr. Josephine Davis Wallace
Dr. Joe Yelderman

The Book Cover, *Invitation to Science*, *World of Science*, and *FUNtastic Facts* features found in this textbook were designed and developed by the National Geographic Society's Education Division.
Copyright © 2000 National Geographic Society

The name "National Geographic Society" and the Yellow Border Rectangle are trademarks of the Society and their use, without prior written permission, is strictly prohibited.

McGraw-Hill School Division
A Division of The McGraw-Hill Companies

Copyright © 2000 McGraw-Hill School Division,
a Division of the Educational and Professional
Publishing Group of The McGraw-Hill Companies, Inc.

All rights reserved. No part of this book may be reproduced or transmitted in any form or by any means, electronic or mechanical, including photocopying, recording, or by any information storage and retrieval system, without permission in writing from the publisher.

McGraw-Hill School Division
Two Penn Plaza
New York, New York 10121

Printed in the United States of America

ISBN 0-02-277434-3 / 2

1 2 3 4 5 6 7 8 9 004/046 05 04 03 02 01 00 99

CONTENTS

UNIT 1 WATERING EARTH'S PLANTS

62127

UNIT 2 · CLUES FROM THE PAST

UNIT 3 CHANGES ALL AROUND

UNIT 4

WATCH IT MOVE

UNIT 5 ROCKY HOMES

UNIT 6

HUMAN BODY: HEART AND LUNGS

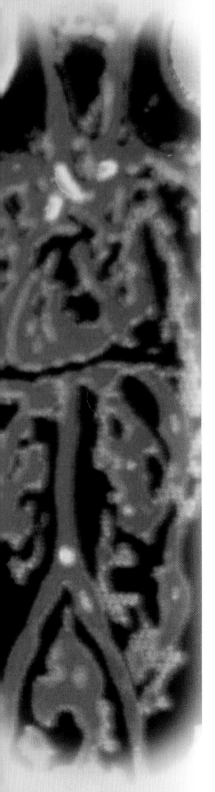

REFERENCE SECTION

ACTIVITIES

READING PICTURES AND CHARTS

FACTS, PROBLEMS, AND PUZZLES

PROBLEMS AND PUZZLES

FUNTASTIC FACTS

YOUR TEXTBOOK at a Glance

Begin each topic with an **Explore** question. Then try an **Explore Activity.**

Topic 5
PHYSICAL SCIENCE

Why it matters

Magnets can pull [some] kinds of things.

...nce Words

...pull

... places on a ...where its pull ...st

...away

All About Magnets

Have you ever held a magnet? The pictures show what happens when you move a magnet close to paper clips.

E X P L O R E

Does this happen to all things that a magnet comes close to?

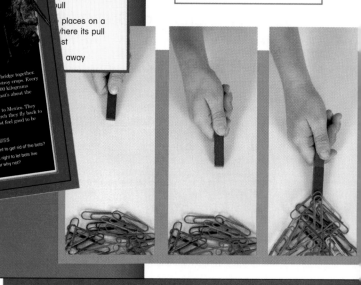

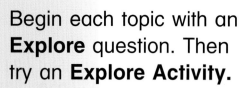

Health Link

NATIONAL GEOGRAPHIC **World of SCIENCE**

SCIENCE MAGAZINE

Liv...

A Closer Look

THE BATS UNDER THE BRIDGE.

Once, only a few bats lived under this bridge in Austin, Texas. Then the city repaired the bridge. There were lots of dark spaces under it. Soon it was home to thousands of bats!

Some people wanted to get rid of the bats. They thought all bats were pests. Other people wanted the bats to stay.

The city let the bats stay. Now more than a million bats live under the bridge each summer!

At night the bats leave the bridge together. They hunt for insects that destroy crops. Every night the bats eat about 13,500 kilograms (30,000 pounds) of insects. That's about the weight of four hippos!

In November, the bats fly to Mexico. They stay there all winter. In March they fly back to the bridge in Austin. It must feel good to be home!

DISCUSS

1. Why did some people want to get rid of the bats?
2. Do you think the city was right to let bats live under the bridge? Why or why not?

Read the **Science Magazines. National Geographic World of Science** is the first magazine in each unit.

Brain Power
Woodpeckers eat bugs

Answer fun questions about real-world facts.

NATIONAL GEOGRAPHIC

FUNtastic Facts

Some habitats are hot and dry. A desert in Chile, in South America, once had no rain for 14 years! What was it like to live there?

EXPLORE ACTIVITY

What will stick to a magnet?

What kind of objects will stick to a magnet? Find out.

What to do

1. Work with 2 partners. Make a fishing pole like this one. Put all the objects in a lunch bag.
2. **Predict** What kind of fish will you catch? Record in the *Science Journal*.
3. Take turns fishing until nothing comes out of the bag. Put your catch in a pile.
4. Put the things left in the bag in another pile.

What did you find out?

1. **Compare** How are the things you caught the same?
2. **Infer** What things will stick to a magnet?

What you need
- paper bag
- metal objects
- nonmetal objects
- ring magnet
- string
- pencil
- *Science Journal*

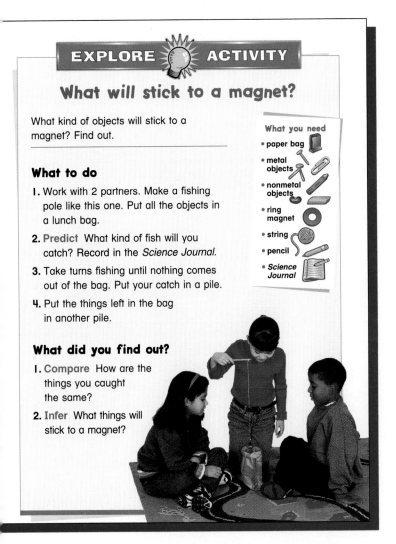

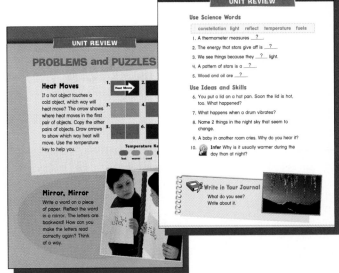

UNIT REVIEW

PROBLEMS and PUZZLES

Heat Moves
If a hot object touches a cold object, which way will heat move? The arrow shows where heat moves in the first pair of objects. Copy the other pairs of objects. Draw arrows to show which way heat will move. Use the temperature key to help you.

Temperature Key
hot   warm   cool

Mirror, Mirror
Write a word on a piece of paper. Reflect the word in a mirror. The letters are backward! How can you make the letters read correctly again? Think of a way.

UNIT REVIEW

Use Science Words

constellation light reflect temperature fuels

1. A thermometer measures ___?___
2. The energy that stars give off is ___?___
3. We see things because they ___?___ light.
4. A pattern of stars is a ___?___
5. Wood and oil are ___?___

Use Ideas and Skills

6. You put a lid on a hot pan. Soon the lid is hot, too. What happened?
7. What happens when a drum vibrates?
8. Name 2 things in the night sky that seem to change.
9. A baby in another room cries. Why do you hear it?
10. **Infer** Why is it usually warmer during the day than at night?

Write in Your Journal
What do you see?
Write about it.

▲ Have fun solving **Problems and Puzzles. Write in Your Journal** about what you learn.

▲ Build your skills with **Skill Builders.** Use the **Handbook** for help.

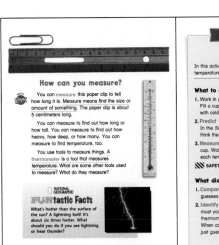

How can you measure?

You can measure this paper clip to tell how long it is. Measure means find the size or amount of something. The paper clip is about 5 centimeters long.

You can measure to find out how long or how tall. You can measure to find out how heavy, how deep, or how many. You can measure to find temperature, too.

You use tools to measure things. A thermometer is a tool that measures temperature. What are some other tools used to measure? What do they measure?

NATIONAL GEOGRAPHIC
FUNtastic Facts
What's hotter than the surface of the sun? A lightning bolt! It's about six times hotter. What should you do if you see lightning or hear thunder?

SKILL BUILDER
Measure

In this activity you will measure the temperature inside 3 cups.

What to do
1. Work in groups of 3. Fill a cup with ice. Fill a cup with warm water. Fill a cup with cold water. Wait 2 minutes.
2. **Predict** Touch the outside of each cup. In the *Science Journal*, write what you think the temperature is for each cup.
3. **Measure** Place a thermometer in each cup. Wait 2 minutes. Find and record each temperature.

SAFETY Handle thermometers carefully.

What you need
- 3 clear plastic cups
- ice cubes
- warm water
- cold water
- 3 thermometers
- clock
- *Science Journal*

What did you find out?
1. **Compare** Were your guesses close?
2. **Identify** When must you use a thermometer? When can you just guess?

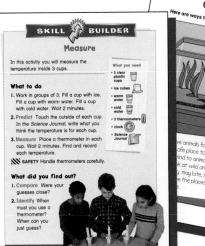

Care of Animals
Here are ways to care for animals.

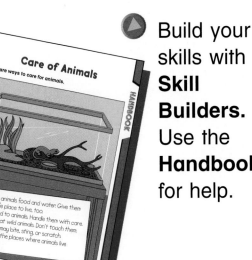

...ve animals food and water. Give them ...afe place to live, too.
...kind to animals. Handle them with care.
...k at wild animals. Don't touch them.
...y may bite, sting, or scratch.
...e the places where animals live.

HANDBOOK

INVITATION TO SCIENCE

Sylvia Earle

Is that a robot in the ocean? No, it's a scientist named Sylvia Earle. She's wearing a special diving suit.

Special diving equipment helps Sylvia breathe underwater.

Like many scientists, Sylvia wants to observe animals in their own homes. To learn about ocean animals, Sylvia stays underwater for long periods of time. Sometimes she wears equipment that lets her breathe underwater. Other times she explores from inside a special submarine, called a submersible. Once, she lived in an underwater laboratory for two weeks!

Sylvia hopes to learn much more about ocean life. She says, "There's so much to explore—from coral reefs in the tropics to the deep canyons and great, untouched mountains that await in the deep sea."

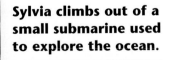

Sylvia climbs out of a small submarine used to explore the ocean.

BE A SCIENTIST

Some people store objects in attics or basements. Some objects may be very old and not used any more. Old objects may tell a story about when they were used. They also may tell a story about the people who used them.

Studying ancient objects helps us learn about the past. *Ancient* is a word that means "very old." An archeologist is a scientist who studies ancient objects.

EXPLORE

These old objects were found in an attic. What are they? How do you think people used them?

EXPLORE ACTIVITY

What can archeologists learn from objects?

In this activity, you'll try to identify an object by looking at only parts of it.

What you need

- magazines
- scissors
- *Science Journal*

What to do

1. Cut a picture of an object out of a magazine. Cut the picture into several pieces.

2. Give a partner some of the pieces to study. Write what the object is in the *Science Journal*.

3. Ask your partner to guess what the whole object is. Write the answer in the *Science Journal*.

4. Take turns. Repeat.

What did you find out?

1. How close was your partner's guess? What clues did your partner use?

2. **Infer** What might archeologists learn from parts of objects?

S5

How do scientists work?

The Explore Activity showed how science is like a puzzle. Scientists try to use what they know to solve the puzzle. Sometimes pieces of the puzzle are missing. How can you tell what the missing pieces look like? It helps to look at the pieces you have and imagine what the missing pieces might look like.

Suppose an archeologist found the skull and leg bones of a dinosaur. These parts would help him guess what the whole dinosaur looked like.

Suppose another found a tooth and tail bones of a dinosaur. That archeologist might need to find more pieces.

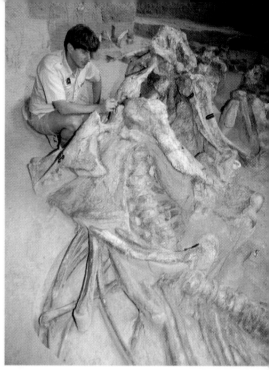

Archeologists study different things. Sometimes they study ancient dinosaur bones. Sometimes they study objects that people used or made. Even an old coin can tell an archeologist a lot about people who lived long ago!

Dr. Ruben Mendoza works at a university in California. He works with students and other archeologists. They work together to look for ancient objects. Archeologists call that part of their job a "dig." They use that word because they dig up old objects from the ground.

Where an object is found is important. Before a dig, archeologists lay lines of string over the dig area. Then they make a paper map showing the same area.

Archeologists mark on the map where each ancient object is found.

How do archeologists know where to dig? Archeologists are like detectives. They look for clues. They might study places where people used to live, but where they no longer do.

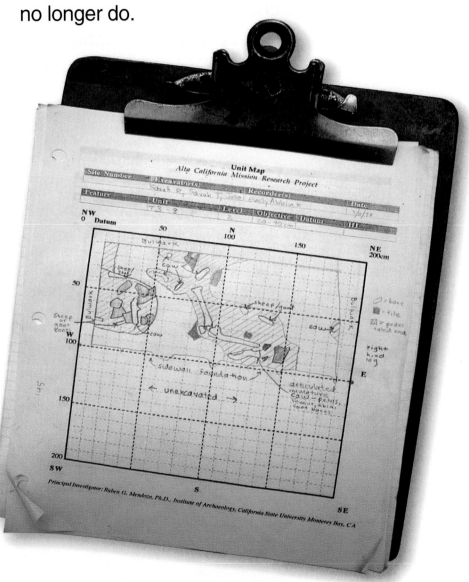

What can scientists learn from ancient objects?

Objects can give information about people who lived long ago—even people who lived thousands of years ago! Sometimes archeologists find arrowheads made of stone. They might find needles made from bones. These objects show that ancient people knew how to make and use tools.

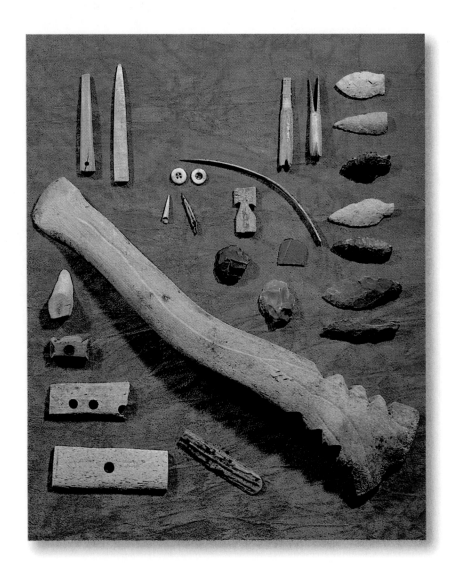

Not all objects are dug up. Sometimes archeologists find ancient drawings on the wall of a cave or cliff. The drawings show things about the people and animals that once lived there.

Archeologists must hold old objects very carefully. The objects might break easily or already be broken.

An archeologist weighs and measures an object and gives it a number. All information is written on a card. The archeologist also writes down the place and date. Even the name of the person who found the object is written down!

This information is stored in a computer. Then other people can read about the objects. The objects are often kept in a museum so many people can see them.

How do scientists work with others?

Sometimes Dr. Mendoza meets with other archeologists to learn more about ancient people and places. Dr. Mendoza also uses the computer to find information people have written about them.

People who are not archeologists also help Dr. Mendoza learn about ancient objects. Students help him to dig, bag and record objects, and draw maps. Dr. Mendoza might ask older people what they know about an object.

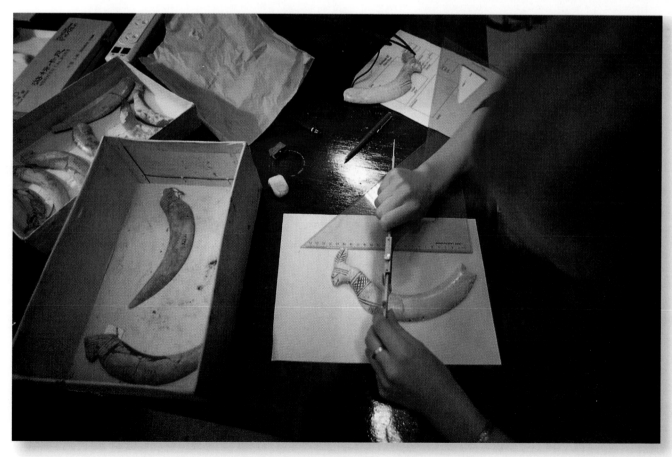

How can I be like a scientist?

Scientists start by asking questions. Archeologists find ancient objects and wonder what they are. Sometimes they just see part of an object. What was it used for? Who made it? Being a scientist means looking for answers to your questions!

In your Explore Activity, you asked a question. What can archeologists learn from objects? You made an activity to answer the question. You and a partner guessed what something was just by seeing part of it. This is what archeologists do. How close were your guesses? You wrote your answers in the *Science Journal* to share with others. This is how a scientist works!

Dr. Mendoza's work shows how important science is. Dr. Mendoza finds information that helps us learn. We can learn about Earth. We can learn about dinosaurs. We can learn about ancient people. Archeology is like the history of people. Learning about ancient people helps us understand about ourselves.

REVIEW

1. How does an archeologist learn about ancient people and how they lived?

2. Draw an archeologist doing part of his or her job.

3. How do archeologists help us learn more about ourselves?

BE A SCIENTIST Glossary

A

ancient very old

archeologist a scientist who studies ancient objects

ask to make up a question you want to find the answer to

C

cause and effect how one thing changes another thing

classify to group things that are alike in some way

communicate to share ideas by talking, writing, or drawing

compare and contrast to look at things to see how they are the same and how they are different

conclude to make a decision based on all the things you know

D

decide to choose from different ideas or things

E

explain to help somebody understand something

G

get information to find out facts about something

I

identify to know something by name

infer to use what you know to figure something out

M

measure to find the size or amount of something

O

observe to use your senses to learn something

P

plan to choose how you are going to do something

predict to guess what is going to happen before an activity

put in order to place things in a way that's easy to use

U

use numbers to show how much there is of something, adding and subtracting

WATERING EARTH'S PLANTS

CHAPTER 1

PLANTS
AND THEIR
PARTS

1

Topic
LIFE SCIENCE
1

Why it matters

Plants have parts that help them to live.

Science Words

roots plant part that grows under the ground

stem holds the plant up straight

leaves plant part that grows from the stem

observe use your senses to learn about something

life cycle a pattern of growth that happens over and over again

Plants Have Parts

Did you know that some plants can grow in dry places? Did you know that some plants can grow in water? Plants can grow when they get the water they need.

EXPLORE

How do plants get the water they need?

How can plants get water?

What part of a plant takes in water?
Find out.

What to do

1. Place both plants in a sunny place.

2. Keep the soil of plant A moist. Wipe the leaves only of plant B each day with a moist sponge.

3. **Observe** After a few days, gently remove plant A from its pot. Use a hand lens. Observe the plant part that grows in the soil. Draw it in the *Science Journal*.

4. Repeat step 3 for plant B.

   SAFETY Wash your hands.

What did you find out?

1. **Compare** What happened to plants A and B? Why?

2. **Infer** What part of a plant takes in water, the leaves, or the roots?

What you need

- 2 small potted plants (labeled A and B)
- water
- sponge
- newspaper
- hand lens
- *Science Journal*

What are the parts of a plant?

All living things need water. The Explore Activity shows how plants get water to live. **Roots** take in water and minerals that the plant needs. Roots are the part of the plant that grows under the ground.

Roots have one more important job. They help to hold the plant in the ground. Why is this important?

NATIONAL GEOGRAPHIC

FUNtastic Facts

Carrots are roots. A Japanese radish is a very big root. You can eat these roots. What are other roots you can eat?

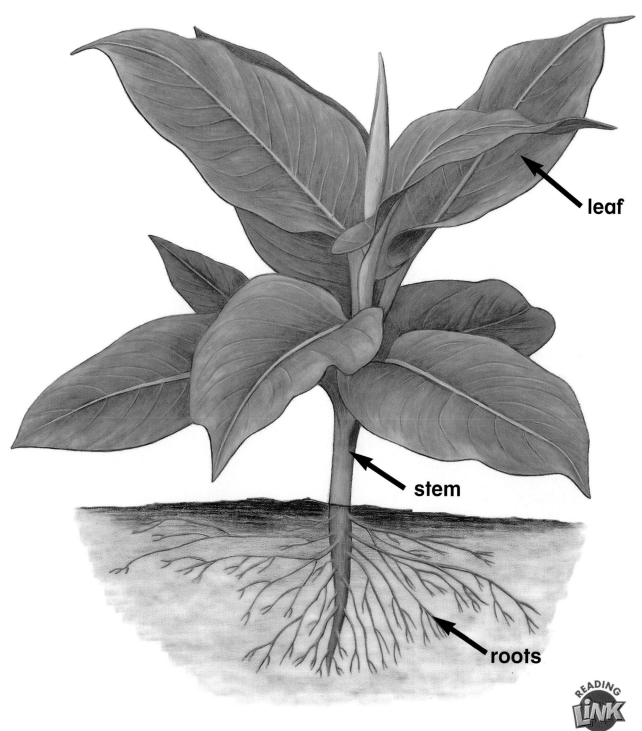

leaf

stem

roots

Water moves from the roots to another part of the plant called the stem. The stem holds the plant up straight. That way its leaves can get sunlight to make food for the plant. Leaves are the part of the plant that grows from the stem.

What can you observe about a plant?

You can learn about plant parts when you **observe** them. Observe means to use your senses to learn about something. You can observe something by hearing, touching, smelling, tasting, or seeing.

It is not always safe to use all of your senses to observe something. You should not taste or touch a plant that you don't know. Why?

You can share what you observe by telling. You can write words. You can also draw a picture. What else can you do?

SKILL BUILDER

Observe

In this activity you will observe a plant. Then you will show what you observed.

What you need

- unpotted plant
- hand lens
- newspaper
- *Science Journal*

What to do

1. **Observe** Look at your plant with a hand lens. Touch it. Smell it.

2. Draw and write what you observe in the *Science Journal*.

 SAFETY Wash your hands.

What did you find out?

1. **Explain** What did you observe?

2. **Identify** Which senses did you use to observe the plant?

What is the life cycle of a plant?

Many kinds of plants grow from seeds. Seeds grow into young plants called seedlings. The seedlings grow into adult plants. Adult plants make new seeds. The adult plants die. What happens to the seeds?

A pattern of growth that happens over and over again is called a life cycle. What other living things have a life cycle? Do non living things have a life cycle?

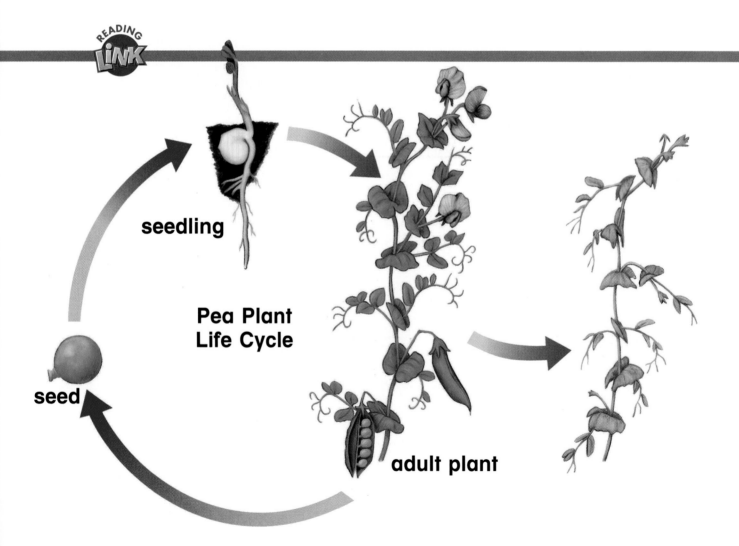

READING LINK

seedling

Pea Plant
Life Cycle

seed

adult plant

People cannot live without plants. People use plants for food, for clothing, and for homes.

REVIEW

1. What are the parts of a plant?

2. What does each plant part do?

3. Why are seeds important to the life cycle of a plant?

4. **Observe** What are some things you can observe about the parts of a tree?

5. **Think and Write** How else do people use plants?

9

Topic
LIFE SCIENCE
2

Why it matters

Fruits are the part of a plant that holds the seeds. The seeds will make more plants like itself.

Science Words

fruit the plant part that holds the seeds

Plants and More Plants

Did you ever watch a bee at a flower? It flies from flower to flower all day long! The flowers are so pretty. They smell so sweet.

EXPLORE

How are flowers different? How are flowers the same?

10

What can you observe about flowers?

You will observe flowers to tell how they are alike and different.

What to do

1. **Observe** Look closely at the flower on the first Picture Card.

2. Write what you observe about the flower's color, shape, and parts in the *Science Journal.*

3. Repeat steps 1 and 2 for the other cards.

What did you find out?

1. **Compare** What was the same about the flowers you observed?

2. **Contrast** What was different about them?

11

Why are flowers and fruits important?

The Explore Activity shows that flowers come in all colors, sizes, and shapes. Many flowers have a smell, too.

Why are there so many different kinds of flowers? Flowers need bees, birds, and other animals to visit them. There's a sweet liquid inside to drink!

Some animals visit flowers of a special color. Some animals visit flowers that smell. Others visit flowers of a special shape.

When an animal visits a flower, it gets covered with powder. Then it visits another flower. Some powder rubs off onto parts of this next flower.

This powder makes seeds grow inside the flower. Then a **fruit** starts to grow around the seeds. A fruit is the part of the plant that holds the seeds. The seeds will make new plants.

What do the new plants look like?

Most fruits have seeds inside. Some fruits have only one seed. Others have many seeds. Yet one seed or many, seeds make new plants.

All new plants grow to look like the same plants the seeds came from. What will grow from these seeds?

Many kinds of plants need animals to help them make fruits and spread seeds. Many kinds of animals need the flowers and fruits of plants for food. This is one way that plants and animals need each other.

REVIEW

1. Why are flowers important?

2. What is a fruit?

3. Why is a fruit important to plants?

4. **Infer** A pepper is a fruit. Why?

5. **Think and Write** Draw your own kind of flower. The flower must catch powder from other flowers that the wind blows.

Why it matters

The parts of a plant help it to live where it does.

Places Plants Live

Have you ever seen plants like these? Look at their leaves. Some leaves are thick. Some leaves are thin. Some leaves are even very sharp!

Each plant lives in a different place. Can you guess where each plant lives?

EXPLORE

How do leaves help plants live where they do?

shady spot
moist soil

full sun
little watering

bright light
some shade

EXPLORE ACTIVITY

How does the shape of a leaf help a plant?

In this activity you will see how leaf shape helps plants keep their water longer.

What you need

- 2 paper towels
- clock
- bowl of water
- wax paper
- scissors
- *Science Journal*

What to do

1. Cut 2 large identical leaf shapes from 2 paper towels. Twist one of the paper towel leaves.

2. Wet both leaves in the bowl of water. Lay the leaves on wax paper.

3. **Observe** Check each leaf every 15 minutes. Record your observations in the *Science Journal*.

What did you find out?

1. **Observe** Which leaf shape stayed wet longer?

2. **Infer** Which leaf would you find in a dry place? Why do you think so?

How can plants live where they do?

This place is very dry. The soil is very sandy. Water does not stay in the soil long. How can plants live here?

Many cacti (KAK tye) have roots that spread out near the top of the soil. That way roots can get water quickly. Other plants have long roots. They get water deep in the ground.

Leaves also help plants live in dry places. The Explore Activity shows how a leaf's shape helps a plant keep its water.

Some plants grow in wet places. The water lily has special parts that grow in water. Its roots are at the bottom of the pond. Its stem is long. It has large, flat leaves that float on the top of the water.

Brain Power

Why is it important for water lily leaves to float on top of the water?

How can plants live in forests?

This forest is cold and snowy in winter. Its soil is dark and moist. Water stays in it longer than in sandy soil.

This is a conifer forest. Conifer leaves look like needles and are small and waxy. The waxy coat helps keep water inside the leaves.

The shape of conifer trees is also special. The shape lets heavy snow fall off branches. Why is this important?

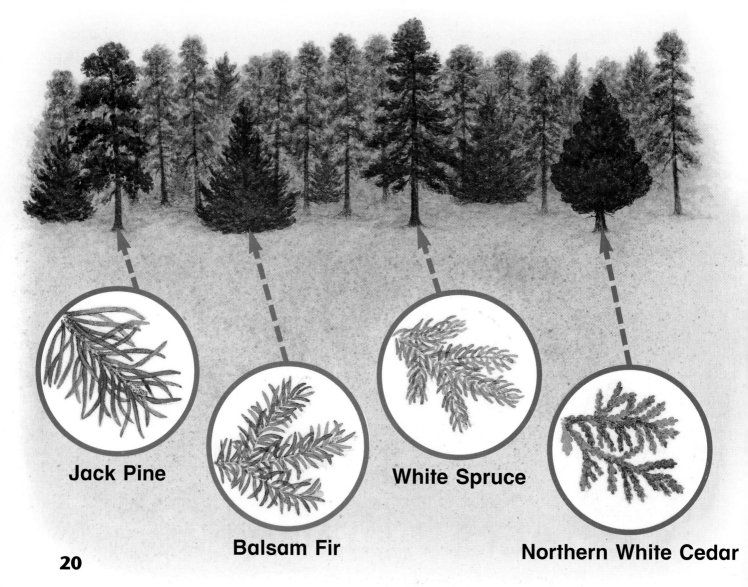

Jack Pine

Balsam Fir

White Spruce

Northern White Cedar

Some plants live where it is wet and shady. Some plants live where it is dry and sunny. You can care for plants if you know what they need to live. How would you care for each plant here?

REVIEW

1. What helps a cactus to live in a hot, dry place?

2. What helps a water lily to live in a wet place?

3. What parts help a conifer to live in a cold, snowy place?

4. **Communicate** Draw a cactus and the place where it lives.

5. **Think and Write** Why can plants live where they do?

World of SCIENCE

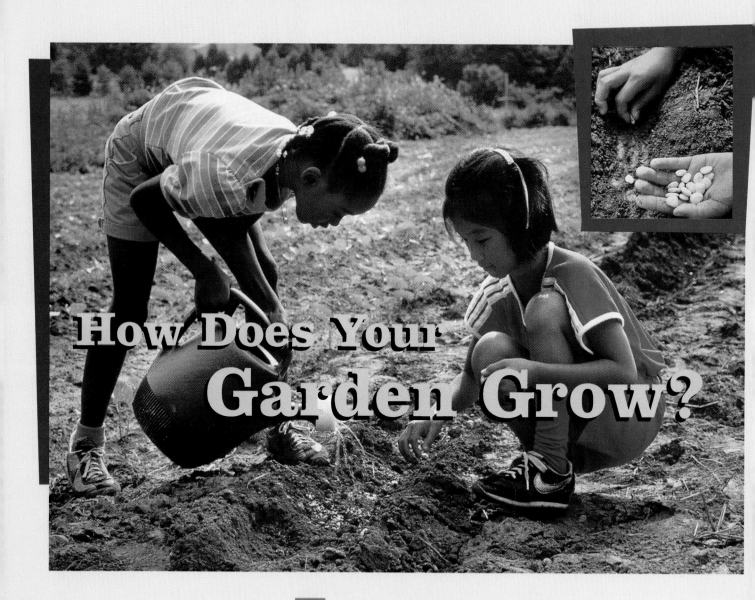

How Does Your Garden Grow?

These children are planting seeds in a garden. What do seeds need to grow? They need soil, sunlight, and water.

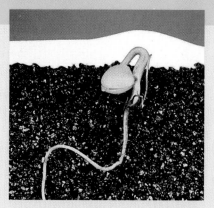

Slowly, a plant will start to grow. The plant makes a root and a stem. Gravity pulls the root down into the soil. The stem grows up toward the light.

Remember to care for your garden. In dry weather, give your plants some water. Don't pull parts off a plant. If you do, the plant may die.

Don't touch poison ivy! You may get an itchy rash.

Discuss

What might happen if a plant doesn't get enough sunlight?

CHAPTER 1 REVIEW

Use Science Words

Match each word with its picture.

1. stem page 5

2. observe page 6

3. roots page 4

4. life cycle page 8

5. leaves page 5

a.

b.

c.

d.

e.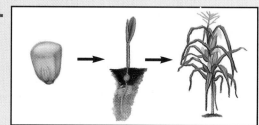

Use Science Ideas

What does each part do for the plant? pages 4–5, 12

6. leaf   7. roots   8. stem   9. fruit

10. **Observe** What helps this live where it does? page 18

PROBLEMS and PUZZLES

Living or not ? How can you tell when something is living or nonliving?

CHAPTER 2
WATER
FOR PLANTS

Why it matters

Earth's water moves between Earth and sky over and over again.

Science Words

evaporates changes to a gas in air

condenses changes from a gas back to a liquid

water cycle the moving of water between Earth and sky over and over again

Water on the Move

Did you ever feel rain fall on your face? Did you ever catch a snowflake on your tongue?

Rain and snow are wet. That is because they are water.

EXPLORE

Water falls from the sky. How does water get up there?

26

Where does the water for rain come from?

You will make a model of Earth and the sky to find out where rain comes from.

What you need

- small cup
- sand
- cup of water
- plastic storage bag
- *Science Journal*

What to do

1. Put some dry sand into a paper cup. Pour some water into the cup.

2. Place the cup into a plastic bag. Seal the bag. Place it in a sunny place.

3. Observe Look at the model Earth and sky each hour for a few hours. In the *Science Journal*, draw any changes.

What did you find out?

1. Observe After a few hours, where did you see water?

2. Infer Where did it come from?

3. Infer Where does the water for rain come from?

27

Where does water go?

The clothes are wet. What will happen to the wet clothes? Where does the water go?

Heat from the Sun changes the water in the clothes. The liquid water **evaporates.** When water evaporates, it changes to a gas in the air that you cannot see.

Water as a gas cools in the air. It **condenses**. When water condenses, it changes from a gas back to a liquid that you can see.

Did water evaporate or condense in the Explore Activity? It did both. First, liquid water in the sand became a gas. It evaporated. Then the water in the air cooled. It became liquid water on the bag. It condensed.

What is the water cycle?

You cannot see water move into the air, but you know that it does. It moves between the ground and the sky and back again. The moving of water between Earth and sky over and over again is called the water cycle.

1 The Sun heats Earth's water. Liquid water from land, oceans, and rivers evaporates into the air.

2 The water in the air cools and condenses. The tiny water drops make clouds.

3 The tiny drops get bigger. Water falls as rain, snow, or hail.

Why it matters

Living things need water from the water cycle to live, but we never know how much water will fall. Why do you think that people build reservoirs?

REVIEW

1. What happens to a puddle on a sunny day?

2. What makes that happen?

3. What happens when a gas condenses?

4. **Communicate** Tell in your own words what the water cycle is.

5. **Think and Write** Draw the water cycle.

Topic 5
EARTH SCIENCE

Why it matters

Weather changes from day to day and from season to season.

Weather Changes

What was the weather like when you left for school this morning? Is the weather the same now as it was this morning? Will the weather be the same tomorrow?

EXPLORE

How do you think weather changes during a day? How do you think weather changes during a week?

How can weather change?

In this activity you will keep track of weather changes.

What you need

• weather chart

• *Science Journal*

What to do

1. **Observe** Observe the weather in the morning, at lunch, and in the afternoon. Do this for 5 days.

2. Show what you observe in the *Science Journal* and weather chart.

3. **Identify** Look for patterns.

What did you find out?

1. **Identify** How did the weather change each day? How did it change during the week?

2. **Compare** Do you see any weather patterns? What are they?

33

What is weather?

The Sun, Earth, air temperature, and water help shape the weather. A change in any of these things means that the weather will be different.

Sometimes there is very little water in the air and the Sun shines. Then the day may be dry and warm.

winter

spring

Sometimes there is a lot of water in the air and it is cloudy. Then the day may be snowy and cold, or rainy.

The Explore Activity shows that weather can change from day to day. It can even change during the day. If you record the weather for a whole year, you will see that it also changes from season to season. Where might it snow or rain here? Tell why.

summer

fall

What are floods and droughts?

Sometimes weather brings too much rain in one place. This can make a flood happen. Other times too little rain falls in one place. This can make a drought happen.

Brain Power

What can floods and droughts do to plants? What can floods and droughts do to animals?

Weather is important to Earth's plants and people. People dress for what the weather is like. Farmers need to know about the weather so they can care for plants and animals. Who else needs to know about the weather?

REVIEW

1. What shapes weather?

2. Why does the weather change?

3. What are some kinds of weather?

4. **Communicate** What is the difference between a flood and a drought?

5. **Think and Write** What can floods do to people?

Why it matters

Earth's water must not be wasted and must be kept clean.

Science Words

natural resources
things that come from Earth

conserve save

pollute make dirty

Taking Care of Water

How many ways do you use water? There are probably too many ways to list!

You brush your teeth with water. You take a bath with water. You may even wash your dog with water. The water you use really adds up.

EXPLORE

How much water do you use each day? Do you think that people can run out of water?

How much water do you use?

Do you think that you could ever run out of water? This activity will help you find out.

What you need

- 2 cups
- 10 chips
- marker
- *Science Journal*

What to do

1. Label 2 cups as shown.

2. Put 10 chips in the *Water* cup. Let the chips be the amount of water you have to use.

3. Remove a chip from the *Water* cup each time you use water today. Put that chip in the *Uses* cup.

What did you find out?

1. **Identify** How many *Water* chips did you have left at the end of the day? Record in the *Science Journal*.

2. **Predict** Do you think people could run out of water? Explain.

39

How can we save water?

Things that come from Earth are called natural resources. Air and water are some natural resources.

Most of Earth's water is found in oceans. This water is too salty to drink. Only a small part of Earth's water is fresh water that we can use. This water is found in lakes, rivers, and streams.

There is only so much fresh water around for people to drink. Like the chips in the Explore Activity, fresh water can be used up.

So we need to **conserve** water. <u>Conserve means save.</u> We conserve water by turning it off when we are not using it. Where is water being wasted here?

How do people pollute water?

Sometimes people put things into water. They **pollute** it. When people pollute water, they make it dirty.

Living things cannot drink polluted water. How do the people here help keep water clean?

42

We need water for many things — for drinking, for washing, for watering our plants. Water is very important to conserve.

Many towns and cities keep track of their water. When there is a drought, there is much less water. Then the town or city may call a water emergency. During a water emergency, people cannot use water for some things. What might they be?

REVIEW

1. Where is Earth's water found?

2. What does conserve mean?

3. What are some ways to keep water clean?

4. **Observe** Name a way you can conserve water in your home.

5. **Think and Write** Why should we conserve water?

Making Water Safe

The water we use may come from streams and lakes. It travels a long way through pipes.

The water may have mud, germs, and chemicals in it. It must be cleaned before we use it. That's why it goes to a water treatment plant!

Now the water is clean. It's ready to go to homes and offices.

1 First, the water is kept in quiet ponds. Mud in the water falls to the bottom.

Some cities keep used water in ponds. The ponds are filled with plants and fish. After a few weeks, the water returns to the water treatment plant.

3 Next, the water flows through sand. It removes any chemicals.

2 Next, the water is sprayed into the air. Sunlight and air help to kill germs.

DISCUSS

1. How is water cleaned?

2. Why is it important to have water treatment plants?

Use Science Words

evaporates

condenses

water cycle

natural resources

conserve

pollute

1. The moving of water between Earth and the sky over and over again is called the ___?___. page 30

2. When water changes into a gas in the air that you cannot see, it ___?___. page 28

3. When water changes from a gas back to a liquid that you can see, it ___?___. page 29

4. When you save water, you ___?___ it. page 41

5. Things, like air and water, that come from Earth are called ___?___. page 40

6. When people make water dirty they ___?___ it. page 42

Use Science Ideas

7. Why is the water cycle important? page 30

8.  **Observe** What is the weather like today? pages 34–35

9. Why should people save water? pages 40–41

10. How do people pollute water? page 42

PROBLEMS and PUZZLES

Weather in a Jar Put hot water in a jar. Put a pan with ice cubes on top of the jar. Shine a flashlight on the side of the jar. What do you see? Write about it.

Use Science Words

	conserve		evaporate	
fruit		pollute		water cycle

1. The movement of water between Earth and sky over and over again is the ___?___.

2. The plant part that holds seeds is the ___?___.

3. Heat makes the water ___?___.

4. To not waste water means to ___?___.

5. When people make water dirty, they ___?___ it.

Use Ideas and Skills

6. Why do some desert plants have deep roots?

7. Why are some conifer leaves waxy?

8. What must people do when there is a drought?

9. **Observe** This bag was left in the Sun. What do you observe happening?

10. In what ways can water become polluted?

 Write in Your Journal

What do you see?
Write about it.

PROBLEMS and PUZZLES

Take a Hike!

During their hike, the Hiking Club took the photos below. Write about the kinds of things the hikers saw each day. Where did the hike start and end? Trace the map. Draw arrows to show the direction of the hike.

Day 1: Yow! The spines really hurt! Where were we?

Day 2: We found lots of these. Where were we?

Day 3: What a great photo! Where were we?

Weather Station

Use a weather station to keep track of your weather. Measure rain with a rain gauge. Measure wind with a wind gauge. Keep track of weather in a diary.

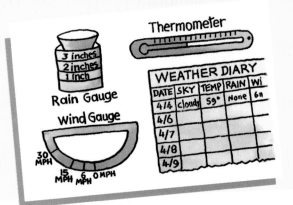

UNIT 2

CLUES FROM THE PAST

CHAPTER 3

FINDING OUT ABOUT THE PAST

Why it matters

Imprints and footprints are clues to the past.

Science Words

imprint a mark that is made when an object presses into something

fossil imprints and remains of things that lived long ago

infer use what you know to figure something out

Using Clues

Do you like puzzles? This picture of a beach is like a puzzle. The footprints are clues. They help to tell about what happened here.

Scientists use clues to tell what happened to the animals and plants of long ago. So can you.

EXPLORE

What do you think happened here? What can you tell from the footprints?

50

What can you learn from footprints?

In this activity you will learn how to "read" footprint clues.

What you need
- ruler
- *Science Journal*

What to do

Your teacher will place cut-out footprints around the classroom.

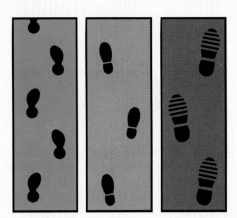

1. **Compare and Contrast** How are the footprints in Sets A and B alike? How are they different? Record in the *Science Journal*.

2. **Compare and Contrast** How are the footprints in Sets A and C alike? How are they different? Record.

What did you find out?

1. **Infer** Were all the footprints made by the same person? Explain.

2. **Identify** Which set of footprints was made by someone walking? Which set was made by someone running?

What clues do we have to the past?

The Explore Activity shows how to read footprints. Scientists read footprints to learn about dinosaurs.

A footprint is a kind of imprint. An imprint is a mark that is made when an object presses into something. Many living things of long ago left imprints. What do these imprints look like?

The bones and teeth of many animals were left behind, too. Imprints and remains of things that lived long ago are **fossils**.

Fossils are clues to animals and plants of the past. Scientists compare fossils to living things today. That's how they can tell how big or small living things were. That's how they can tell what an animal ate.

These are the fossil bones of a Triceratops (trye SER uh tops). It used its teeth to chew plants. It was about as tall as two children.

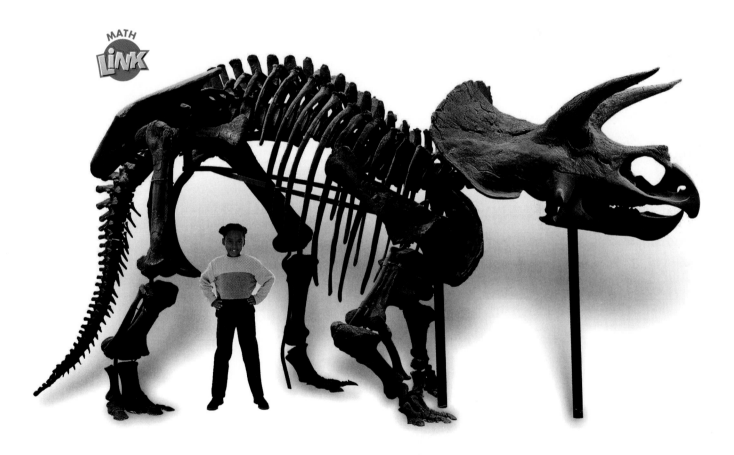

About how tall is this Triceratops? How could you find out?

What shape made this imprint?

Which of these shapes made the imprint below? How can you tell?

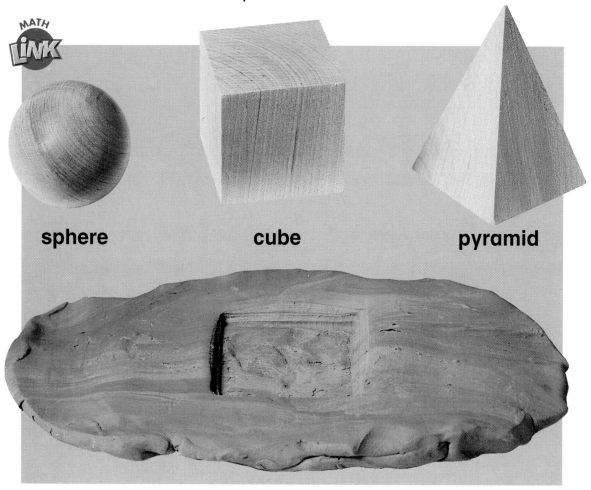

sphere   cube   pyramid

You can use your senses to observe the imprint. You can see the imprint. You use your eyes to see.

How can you tell what made the imprint? You can **infer** what made it. Infer means to use what you know to figure something out.

When scientists observe imprints, they infer what made the imprints.

SKILL BUILDER

Infer from What You Observe

In this activity you will infer what made an imprint.

What you need
- clay
- small objects
- *Science Journal*

What to do

1. Get 3 objects. Flatten some clay. Press each object into the clay. Don't let others see you.

2. **Infer** Let a friend tell what objects made the imprints.

3. **Change It** Try to make 3 different imprints with one object. Let a friend tell what made the imprints.

What did you find out?

1. **Infer** How did you match an imprint with its object?

2. **Explain** Was it ever hard to match an imprint with its object? Explain it in the *Science Journal*.

How did some fossils form?

This fish lived in the sea long ago. How could its remains last until today?

1 The fish died and fell to the bottom. Over time, it was covered by layers of sand.

2 The soft parts of the fish rotted away. Bones and teeth remained.

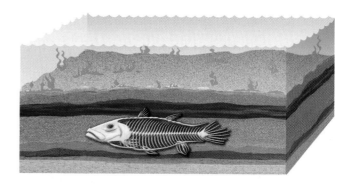

3 Earth changed. After a long time, the water dried up.

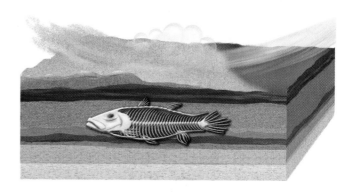

4 Slowly the remains of the fish changed to rock. It became a fossil. The fossil fish was uncovered.

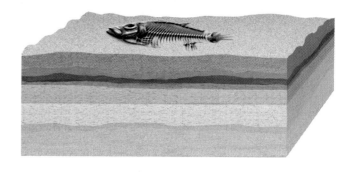

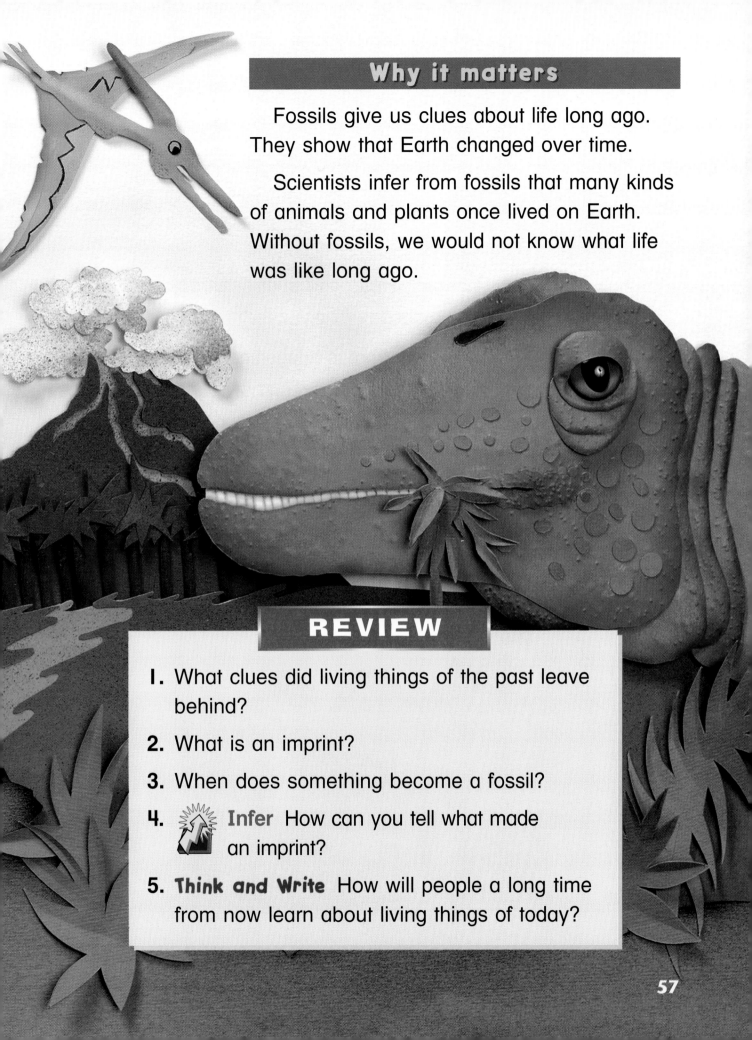

Fossils give us clues about life long ago. They show that Earth changed over time.

Scientists infer from fossils that many kinds of animals and plants once lived on Earth. Without fossils, we would not know what life was like long ago.

REVIEW

1. What clues did living things of the past leave behind?

2. What is an imprint?

3. When does something become a fossil?

4. **Infer** How can you tell what made an imprint?

5. **Think and Write** How will people a long time from now learn about living things of today?

57

Topic 2
LIFE SCIENCE

Why it matters

Fossils don't tell us everything about how dinosaurs lived. Animals that live today give us clues, too.

Animals of Long Ago and Today

Have you ever seen animals like these? These are musk oxen.

What is happening in the picture? The musk oxen know a wolf is nearby. The adults circle around their young.

EXPLORE

Why do you think the adults circle their young?

How do musk oxen keep young safe?

In this activity you will find out why musk oxen circle their young.

What you need

- clock or watch
- *Science Journal*

What to do

1. Play in a large space for 5 minutes.

2. Let most children be adult musk oxen. Let a few children be young musk oxen. Let 3 or 4 children be wolves.

3. Adults circle around the young as shown.

4. Wolves try to get past adults to take a young animal. Adults try to keep wolves from getting in the circle.

What did you find out?

1. **Explain** Was it hard for wolves to get the young? Explain in the *Science Journal*.

2. **Infer** Why do some animals group together?

young   wolf   adult

59

What can fossils tell us about dinosaurs?

Scientists found many fossil bones on a plain in North America. They were the bones of many kinds of dinosaurs. No baby dinosaur bones were found.

Then scientists found fossil eggs. Inside some eggs were tiny dinosaur bones. These fossils show that some kinds of dinosaurs laid eggs.

The eggs were partly covered with mud. Maybe the mud helped the eggs to hatch.

Many nests were found together. The Explore Activity shows how staying in a group helps to keep young animals safe. Maybe these dinosaurs laid their eggs together to keep them safe. Maybe some kinds of dinosaurs cared for their young.

NATIONAL GEOGRAPHIC

FUNtastic Facts

Some dinosaurs laid eggs as small as golf balls. Some dinosaurs laid eggs as large as soccer balls. Can you name some animals today that also lay eggs?

dinosaur eggs in a nest

What clues do animals today give us?

Scientists don't know for sure how dinosaurs lived. They use more than fossil clues. Scientists also get ideas by looking at animals that live today.

Some birds today use nesting grounds. In nesting grounds, birds can hatch and grow safely.

The alligator covers its nest with plants. As the plants rot, they give off heat. The heat helps the eggs to hatch.

These dinosaur footprints look as if a herd, or group, made them. We think some dinosaurs moved in herds because many animals do today.

REVIEW

1. What fossils were found on a plain in North America?

2. Why do scientists think some dinosaurs covered their nests with mud?

3. How do scientists get ideas about how dinosaurs lived?

4. **Observe** What can you observe about animals today?

5. **Think and Write** In what ways might dinosaurs be like animals today?

63

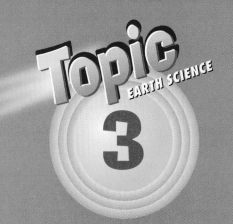

Topic
EARTH SCIENCE
3

Why it matters

We know what dinosaurs looked like from their bones.

Science Words

skeleton a body frame made of bones

paleontologist a person who studies life in the past

Putting the Pieces Together

Can you feel bones under your skin? All your bones make up your skeleton. Your skeleton holds your body together. It gives you shape.

Dinosaurs had skeletons, too. Scientists don't always find a dinosaur's whole skeleton. They usually find only some of its bones.

EXPLORE

What can dinosaur bones tell us about dinosaurs?

64

Which bones fit together?

See how bone clues help you make a dinosaur skeleton.

What you need

- scissors
- tape
- large sheet of paper
- copy of dinosaur bones
- *Science Journal*

What to Do

1. **Infer** Fit the dinosaur bones together. Show your teacher.

2. Tape the bones together. Then tape them to a sheet of paper.

3. **Compare** Trace a line around your dinosaur. Find your dinosaur on pages 67–68. Write its name on your paper.

What did you find out?

1. **Explain** How did you tell which bones fit together?

2. **Infer** What can the skeleton tell you about the dinosaur?

What were dinosaurs like?

A **skeleton** is a body frame made of bones. The Explore Activity shows how bones, when put together, make a skeleton. You used what you know about animals living today. That's how a **paleontologist** (pale ee uhn TOL uh jist) works. A paleontologist is a person who studies life in the past.

Paleoentologists put bones together that they have found to tell what shape a dinosaur was. Then they try to tell what it looked like and how it lived.

Parasaurolophus

(par uh SAWR ahl uh fus)

- It was about 10 meters (33 feet) long.

- It had as many as 300 cheek teeth.

- Its long, bony crest may have helped it make sound.

- It traveled in herds.

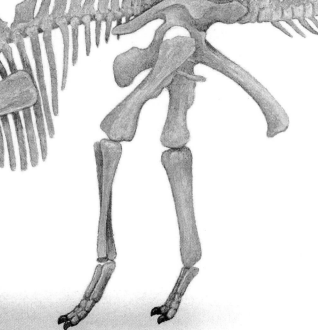

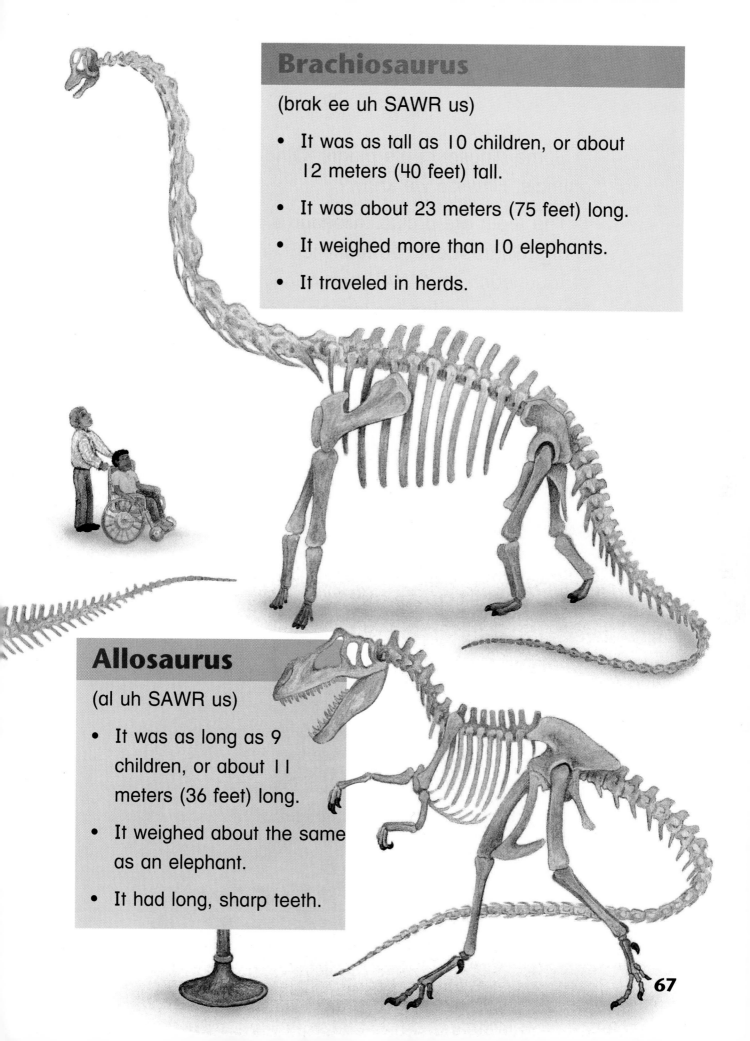

Brachiosaurus

(brak ee uh SAWR us)

- It was as tall as 10 children, or about 12 meters (40 feet) tall.

- It was about 23 meters (75 feet) long.

- It weighed more than 10 elephants.

- It traveled in herds.

Allosaurus

(al uh SAWR us)

- It was as long as 9 children, or about 11 meters (36 feet) long.

- It weighed about the same as an elephant.

- It had long, sharp teeth.

67

What can fossil teeth tell us?

Some dinosaurs ate plants. Others ate animals. How do we know?

The teeth are a clue. Allosaurus teeth were sharp. Sharp teeth can tear meat. The teeth of Iguanodon (ih GWAH nuh dahn) were flat. Flat teeth can grind the leaves of plants. What animals today have teeth shaped like these? What do they eat?

Allosaurus

Iguanodon

The animals of long ago had the same needs that animals have today. They needed food. Maybe they needed *shelter*, too. Shelter is a place where animals can be safe from their enemies.

REVIEW

1. What do paleontologists do?

2. What do we learn from dinosaur skeletons?

3. What do we learn from dinosaur teeth?

4. **Infer** What did the animals of long ago need to live?

5. **Think and Write** Draw the teeth of a dinosaur that ate meat.

Why it matters

The animals of long ago got food the same way that animals do today.

Science Words

food chain how energy from food passes from one living thing to another

Food for Energy

Do you like milk? Do you like peanut butter and jelly sandwiches? How about an apple? These are just some foods you might eat during the day. Which of these foods come from plants? Which come from animals?

EXPLORE

What other foods come from plants and animals?

Where do our foods come from?

In this activity you will classify some foods you eat.

What you need
- crayons
- *Science Journal*

What to do

1. What healthful breakfast would you like to eat? Draw it in the *Science Journal*.

2. **Classify** Which of those foods come from plants? Write or draw them on the chart.

3. **Classify** Which of those foods come from animals? Write or draw them on the chart.

What did you find out?

Explain Where do our foods come from?

What did dinosaurs eat?

The Explore Activity shows that we eat plants and animals. Food gives us the energy we need to live. All living things need energy to live.

Plants get energy from the Sun. They use the Sun's light to make their own food.

Animals can't make their own food. How do you think dinosaurs got energy?

Some dinosaurs got energy by eating plants. Ankylosaurus (ang kile uh SAWR us) was just one kind of plant-eater. Can you name others?

energy

energy

How did meat-eaters get energy?

Some dinosaurs got energy by eating other animals. How energy from food passes from one living thing to another is called a food chain.

Tyrannosaurus (ti ran uh SOR us) was just one kind of meat-eater. Can you name others?

What animals today eat plants? What animals today eat meat?

energy

energy

energy

Why it matters

All living things need energy to live. Plants of long ago used energy from the Sun to make food, just as plants do today. Animals got energy when they ate plants or ate plant-eaters. How do living things get energy today?

REVIEW

1. Why do living things need energy?

2. Where do living things get energy?

3. What is a food chain?

4. **Infer** What might happen to food chains if there was less sunlight?

5. **Think and Write** Draw a food chain that shows animals that live today.

World of SCIENCE

O. C. Marsh

Edward Drinker Cope

The Bone Hunters

Hadrosaur

Edward Drinker Cope and O. C. Marsh were scientists. They hunted for dinosaur bones in the United States in the late 1800s. Instead of working together, each wanted to be the first to find new fossils.

Marsh was the first to find bones of Stegosaurus (STEG-uh-SORE-uhs). Marsh also found bones of flying animals called pterodactyls (ter-uh-DAK-tuls).

Pterodactyls

Cope found bones of *Camara-saurus* (kam-AIR-uh-SORE-uhs) and many other dinosaurs.

Cope and Marsh helped people learn about dinosaurs. The fossils Cope and Marsh found are in museums today.

Stegosaurus

Discuss

1 What might have happened if Cope and Marsh had worked together?

2 How do scientists help each other today?

Use Science Words

fossils
imprints
infer
skeleton
paleontologist
food chain

1. When you use what you know to figure something out, you ___?___. page 54

2. Remains of things that lived long ago are ___?___. page 53

3. Marks left when objects press in something are ___?___. page 52

4. How food energy passes from one living thing to another is called a ___?___. page 74

5. A body frame of bones is a ___?___. page 66

6. A person who studies life in the past is a ___?___. page 66

Use Science Ideas

7. What do scientists learn from footprints? page 52

8. Why do scientists think that some dinosaurs used nesting grounds? page 61

9. What is learned from fossil teeth? page 68

10. **Infer** What can you infer from this picture? page 55

PROBLEMS and PUZZLES

Cool Cat The saber-toothed cat died out long ago. What can you probably say about it? Use what you know about cats today.

CHAPTER 4
EARTH'S SCRAPBOOK

Why it matters

Earth and its living things have changed through time.

Science Words

era a very long amount of time

Paleozoic era time from which the oldest plant and animal fossils have been found

extinct to die out

Mesozoic era the "Age of Reptiles"

Cenozoic era the "Age of Mammals"

Life Long Ago

Do you leave your clothes laying around your room? Or do you place them in a hamper?

Every day Kelsey puts her clothes in the hamper. By the end of a week, there's a tall pile.

EXPLORE

Where are the clothes Kelsey wore on Tuesday? Where are the clothes she wore on Friday? Which of Kelsey's clothes were put in the hamper first?

| Saturday |
| Friday |
| Thursday |
| Wednesday |
| Tuesday |
| Monday |

Which layer is youngest?

In this activity you will show how Earth's layers of rock are stacked.

What to do

1. Press the shell gently into the center of the red clay. Place yellow clay on top.

2. Press the key into the center of the yellow clay. Place green clay on top.

3. Press the button into the center of the green clay. Place blue clay on top.

4. Cut the "sandwich" to see the objects. Draw them in your *Science Journal.*

What you need

- clay strips (red, yellow, blue, green)

- crayons (red, yellow, blue, green)

- plastic knife

- seashell

- button

- key

- *Science Journal*

What did you find out?

1. **Identify** The bottom clay strip is the oldest layer. Which layer is youngest?

2. **Infer** The objects are like fossils in rocks. Which object is the oldest fossil?

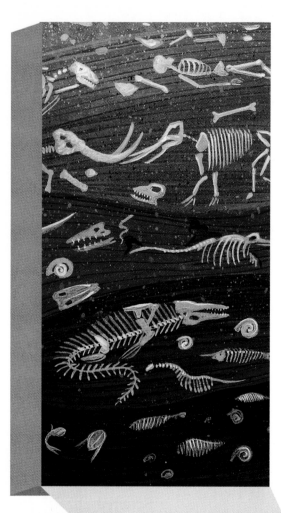

How do we know about Earth's history?

Earth's layers are like a big scrapbook. They hold clues to how Earth has changed over time. As the Explore Activity shows, the layers at the top are younger. The layers at the bottom are older.

Scientists put together clues to explain Earth's history. Each part of Earth's history is called an **era**. An era is a very long amount of time.

Cenozoic
Era

Mesozoic
Era

Paleozoic
Era

A very long time ago, places on Earth may have looked like this. The oldest plant and animal fossils found are from the **Paleozoic** (pay lee uh ZOH ik) **era**. Earth was warm then and there were many seas.

In time Earth changed. It became cooler. Many seas dried up. Many living things could not live when Earth changed. They became **extinct**. Extinct means to die out.

Cenozoic
Era

Mesozoic
Era

Paleozoic
Era

What came next?

The next era was the Mesozoic mez uh ZOH ik) era. The Mesozoic era is called the "Age of Reptiles." During this time, Earth became warmer. There were many swamps and forests. Dinosaurs lived during this era. Other animals lived then, too.

The Cenozoic (see nuh ZOH ik) era came next. It is called the "Age of Mammals". This is the era we live in today, but it started long ago.

The history of Earth is all about change. Through the eras, Earth became warmer or cooler. Some animals and plants kept living. Others became extinct. Do you think that Earth is done changing? Explain.

REVIEW

1. How do scientists know that Earth has changed over time?

2. What is an era?

3. In which era did the dinosaurs live?

4. **Use Numbers** Write Earth's eras in order. Start with the oldest era.

5. **Think and Write** Are dinosaurs extinct? How do you know?

Topic
LIFE SCIENCE
6

Why it matters

Earth's living things become extinct, even today.

Science Words

endangered living things close to becoming extinct

Life Today

What do these young birds need to live? What would happen if they didn't get those things?

EXPLORE

What happens to animals when they don't get the things they need to live?

EXPLORE ACTIVITY

A Game of Needs

What happens to animals when their needs are not met?

What you need

- oaktag
- *Science Journal*

What to do

1. Play in a large open place. Listen as your teacher explains the game.

2. Have "recorders" write information on a large chart for each of the 4 rounds.

3. Copy the information from the large chart in the *Science Journal* at the end of the game.

What did you find out?

1. **Identify** What happens to the number of animals as you play the game?

2. **Infer** What happens to animals when their needs are not met?

food   water   shelter

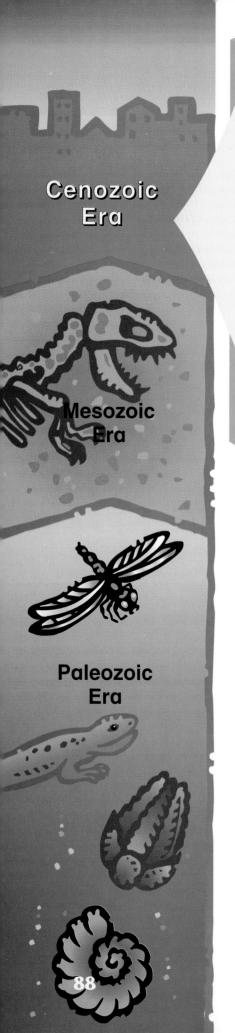

Cenozoic
Era

Mesozoic
Era

Paleozoic
Era

88

Is Earth's history still going on?

The Explore Activity shows that animals can become extinct when their needs are not met. Dinosaurs became extinct when their needs were not met.

Dinosaurs were not the only animals ever to die out. The picture shows some animals from the Cenozoic era. Which are extinct?

Gastric brooding frog

Dusky seaside sparrow

Living things become extinct, even today, when they can't live with changes on Earth. Some changes, like sickness, are natural changes. Others, like changes to plant and animal homes, happen because of people.

Brain Power

The animals in these pictures are extinct. Can you name some others?

What is endangered?

Many plants and animals today are close to becoming extinct because changes on Earth make it hard for them to live. <u>Living things that are close to becoming extinct are endangered</u>.

Pitcher plants are endangered. Building has changed their home too much.

West Indian manatees are endangered, too. Today, people change their ocean homes.

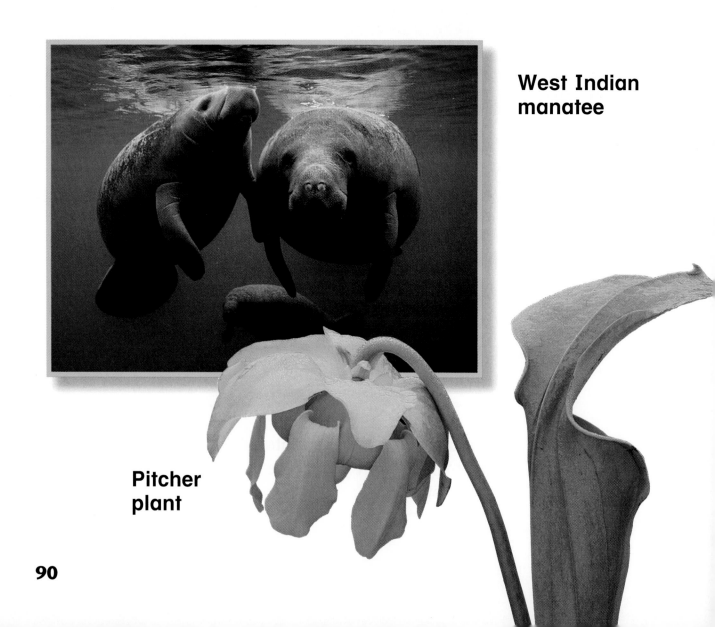

West Indian manatee

Pitcher plant

We need to keep endangered plants and animals safe. We need to keep the places where they live safe. If we don't, endangered plants and animals may become extinct, just like the dinosaurs.

REVIEW

1. When do living things become extinct?

2. Name an extinct animal.

3. Name a kind of plant or animal that is endangered.

4. **Infer** Pandas eat a grass called bamboo. What would happen to pandas if all the bamboo died?

5. **Think and Write** What may happen to people if plants and animals become extinct?

Learning from

Do you ever make mistakes? So can paleontologists! They're the scientists who put dinosaur bones together.

In 1840, scientists discovered the bones of an iguanodon (ih GWAH nuh dahn). One bone looked like a spike. Scientists put it on the dinosaur's nose.

Later, other iguanodons were found. Scientists saw where the spike really belonged. It was the dinosaur's thumb!

Scientists once thought dinosaurs dragged their tails and walked like lizards. Lizards walk with their feet apart. Then scientists looked at dinosaur footprints. No tail marks were found. Dinosaurs really walked with their tails off the ground!

Scientists no longer think dinosaurs walked like lizards. The creatures walked with their feet under them.

DISCUSS

1. What two mistakes did scientists make about dinosaurs?

2. Do you think that scientists may make more mistakes about dinosaurs? Explain.

MISTAKES

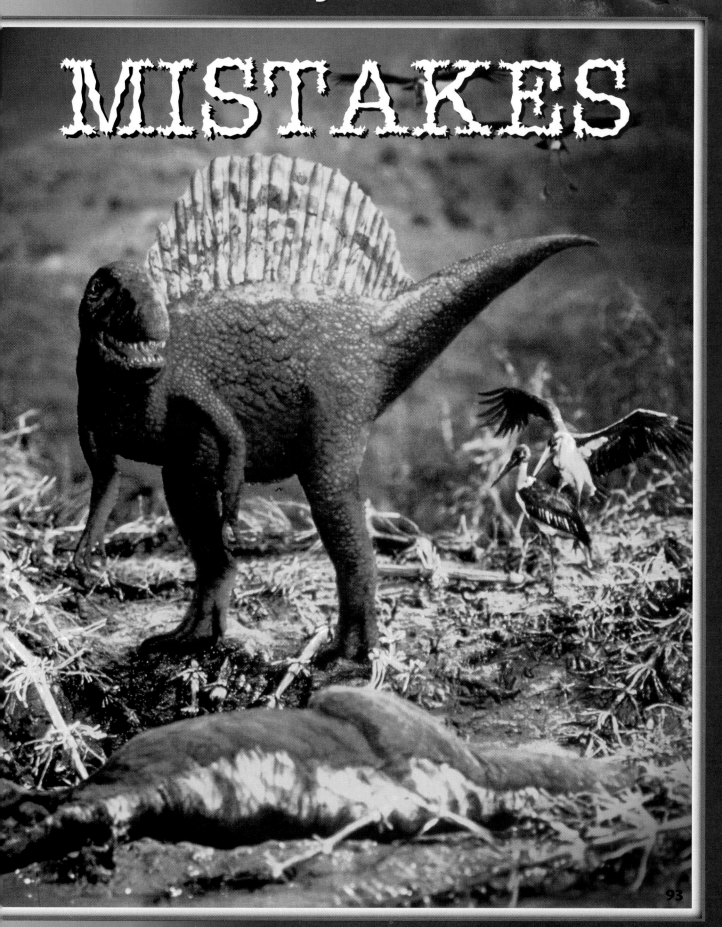

Use Science Words

era

Cenozoic era

endangered

Mesozoic era

extinct

1. The era we live in today is the ___?___. page 84

2. Plants and animals close to becoming extinct are ___?___. page 90

3. A long, long amount of time is an ___?___. page 82

4. The era that is called the "Age of Reptiles" is the ___?___. page 84

5. Living things that die out become ___?___. page 83

Use Science Ideas

6. What is found in the layers of Earth's rocks? page 82

7. The oldest plant and animal fossils found are from which era? page 83

8. What is the Cenozoic era called? page 84

9. Why did dinosaurs become extinct? page 88

10. **Communicate** How are endangered plants and animals different from extinct plants and animals? pages 88–90

PROBLEMS and PUZZLES

Hanging On Draw an endangered animal. Write about why it is endangered. Write a plan to help save it.

Use Science Words

| endangered | extinct | food chain | fossil | skeleton |

1. A dinosaur's footprint is a kind of ___?___.

2. Only a few pandas live today. They are ___?___.

3. The bones in your body make up your ___?___.

4. Energy from food passes from one living thing to another in a ___?___.

5. Dinosaurs died long ago, so they are ___?___.

Use Ideas and Skills

6. Name 2 things paleontologists use to infer about extinct animals.

7. Give one reason that scientists infer some dinosaurs may have laid their eggs in nests.

8. What can you infer from an animal's teeth?

9. Why do living things become extinct?

10. **Infer** A fish fossil is found in a layer of rock below a layer of rock with a dinosaur fossil. Which is older, the fish or the dinosaur?

 Write in Your Journal

What do you see?
Write about it.

PROBLEMS and PUZZLES

Tweetie Island Birds

This graph shows the number of birds counted at Tweetie Island for a few years.

Copy the graph. Look for a pattern. Can you predict the number of birds for the year 2000? Show it on your graph. Talk about it.

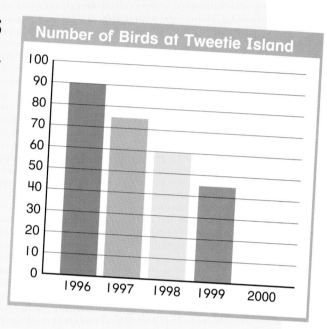

Number of Birds at Tweetie Island

Endangered Animal Fact Cards

Make a fact card of an endangered animal that you choose. Find out about the animal in books and magazines. Draw the animal. Write information about the animal on your card. Share your card with others.

Blue Whale
where it lives: World's oceans
why endangered: hunting
Food: krill

The blue whale is the largest animal that has ever lived.

UNIT 3

CHANGES ALL AROUND

CHAPTER 5

HEAT

Why it matters

Heat can make things change.

Science Words

heat energy that can make things change

temperature how warm or cold something is

measure to find the size or amount of something

thermometer a tool that measures temperature

fuel things that give off heat when they burn

Heat and Change

Have you ever played in the snow? You may know that snow is frozen water.

You may know that snow doesn't last forever. It changes.

EXPLORE

What is changing here? What makes it change?

EXPLORE ACTIVITY

What makes ice cubes change?

Does where you place an ice cube make a difference in how quickly it changes? In this activity you will find out.

What you need

- 3 ice cubes
- 3 cups
- clock
- *Science Journal*

What to do

1. Write your name on each cup. Place an ice cube in each cup.

2. Put one cup in a sunny place. Put one in a shady place. Put one in a warm place.

3. **Observe** Wait 5 minutes. See what happens in each cup. Wait 5 more minutes. See what happens.

What did you find out?

1. **Identify** How did the ice change after 5 minutes? After 10 minutes?

2. **Contrast** In which cup did the ice change most? Why did this happen? Explain in the *Science Journal*.

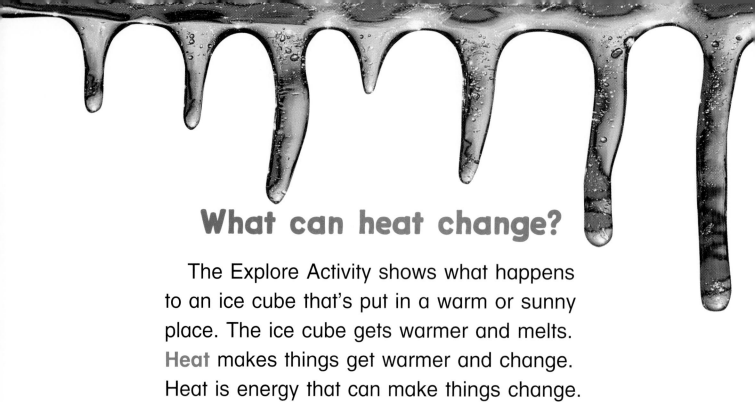

What can heat change?

The Explore Activity shows what happens to an ice cube that's put in a warm or sunny place. The ice cube gets warmer and melts. **Heat** makes things get warmer and change. Heat is energy that can make things change.

Heat can change a solid ice cube into liquid water. Heat makes ice cubes melt. What other solids can heat change to liquids?

Heat can also make liquids change. Heat from the Sun changes the water in puddles. The water dries up, or evaporates. It becomes a gas in the air.

Warm things are hotter than cold things. Temperature tells how warm or cold something is. What things might have a warm temperature? What things might have a cold temperature?

How can you measure?

You can **measure** this paper clip to tell how long it is. Measure means find the size or amount of something. The paper clip is about 5 centimeters long.

You can measure to find out how long or how tall. You can measure to find out how heavy, how deep, or how many. You can measure to find temperature, too.

You use tools to measure things. A **thermometer** is a tool that measures temperature. What are some other tools used to measure? What do they measure?

NATIONAL GEOGRAPHIC

FUNtastic Facts

What's hotter than the surface of the sun? A lightning bolt! It's about six times hotter. What should you do if you see lightning or hear thunder?

SKILL BUILDER

Measure

In this activity you will measure the temperature inside 3 cups.

What you need

- 3 clear plastic cups
- ice cubes
- warm water
- cold water
- 3 thermometers
- clock
- Science Journal

What to do

1. Work in groups of 3. Fill a cup with ice. Fill a cup with warm water. Fill a cup with cold water. Wait 2 minutes.

2. **Predict** Touch the outside of each cup. In the *Science Journal*, write what you think the temperature is for each cup.

3. **Measure** Place a thermometer in each cup. Wait 2 minutes. Find and record each temperature.

    **SAFETY** Handle thermometers carefully.

What did you find out?

1. **Compare** Were your guesses close?

2. **Identify** When must you use a thermometer? When can you just guess?

Where do we get heat from?

Much of our heat is from the Sun's energy. The Sun warms Earth's air, water, and land.

Heat also comes from **fuels**. Fuels are things that give off heat when they burn. Wood, coal, natural gas, and oil are some kinds of fuels. What kinds of fuels do you see here?

Many places on Earth get very cold. You could not live in these places without heat. How is heat used here?

REVIEW

1. What makes ice cream melt and liquids evaporate?

2. What are some things that give us heat?

3. What are fuels?

4. **Measure** What is the temperature of your classroom?

5. **Think and Write** What would Earth be like without the Sun?

Why it matters

Heat can move
through things.

Heat on the Move

Have you ever cooked marshmallows over a fire? It makes them taste great. Why do these people use such long sticks to cook them? How can the marshmallows cook when they're not in the fire?

EXPLORE

Does heat move? Does heat move through all things the same way?

EXPLORE ACTIVITY

Where will heat move first?

In this activity you will observe how heat moves in 3 different containers.

What you need

- hot tap water
- foam cup with lid
- paper cup with lid
- metal can with lid
- clock
- *Science Journal*

What to do

1. Your teacher will pour hot water into 3 containers and cover each with a lid.

2. **Predict** Which container do you think will feel warm first? Write your prediction in the *Science Journal.*

3. Wait a minute. Feel the outside of each container. Record your observations.

What did you find out?

1. **Compare and Contrast** How did each container feel after a minute?

2. **Infer** If you want to keep a drink warm, which container should you use? Why?

107

Where can heat move?

Have you ever picked up a mug of warm milk? Did the handle feel warm, too? Do you know why?

Heat moves from the warm liquid milk to the cooler mug. It moves through the solid mug and warms it. When you touch the mug, the heat moves from the warm mug to your cooler hand. Heat always moves from warmer things to cooler things.

The Explore Activity shows that heat moves through some things more easily than through other things. What happens when you put a metal spoon in hot soup? The spoon gets warm right away. That's because heat moves easily through most metals.

What happens when you put a spoon with a wooden handle in hot soup? The handle stays cool. Why?

Can heat move through air?

The man warms a marshmallow over the fire. How does heat get from the fire to the marshmallow? It moves through the air! When have you felt heat moving through air?

Sometimes heat that moves can burn you. Knowing how heat moves can help keep you safe. How does this person keep heat from burning him?

REVIEW

1. Through what can heat move?

2. Does heat move to cooler things or to warmer things?

3. You hold a cooked hamburger on a bun. Where does the heat move?

4. **Infer** Why do many pots and pans have wooden handles?

5. **Think and Write** Draw a drinking cup that would keep your hand from getting hot. What would you use to make it?

ART
LINK

Keeping Warm

How do birds stay warm in cold weather? The answer is in their feathers. Birds have different kinds of feathers. One kind is called down. Down feathers are small and soft. They grow all over a bird's body.

Life Science Link

Down feathers form a soft, loose layer around a bird. Heat from the bird gets trapped in the down. The trapped warm air helps the bird stay warm.

Layers of clothes that people wear work like down feathers. Warm air from our bodies gets trapped in the layers of clothes. The trapped air helps us stay warm.

Down keeps people warm, too. We put down inside coats, quilts, sleeping bags, and many other things.

Discuss

1 How do down feathers keep birds warm?

2 Do you have any clothes that contain down?

Use Science Words

Match each word with its meaning.

1. heat	**a.** find the size or amount of something page 102
2. temperature	**b.** energy that can make things change page 100
3. measure	**c.** how warm or cold something is page 101
4. fuels	**d.** a tool to measure temperature page 103
5. thermometer	**e.** things that give off heat when they burn page 104

Use Science Ideas

6. How can adding heat change liquids? page 101

7. How can adding heat change solids? page 100

8. What are some kinds of fuels? page 104

9. You stand near an oven. Why do you feel heat? page 110

10. **Measure** Find the temperature of your school yard. page 103

PROBLEMS and PUZZLES

Heating Up Get 2 cans. Wrap one with black paper. Put the same amount of water in each can. Put them in sunlight. What will the water temperatures be after 5 minutes? Find out.

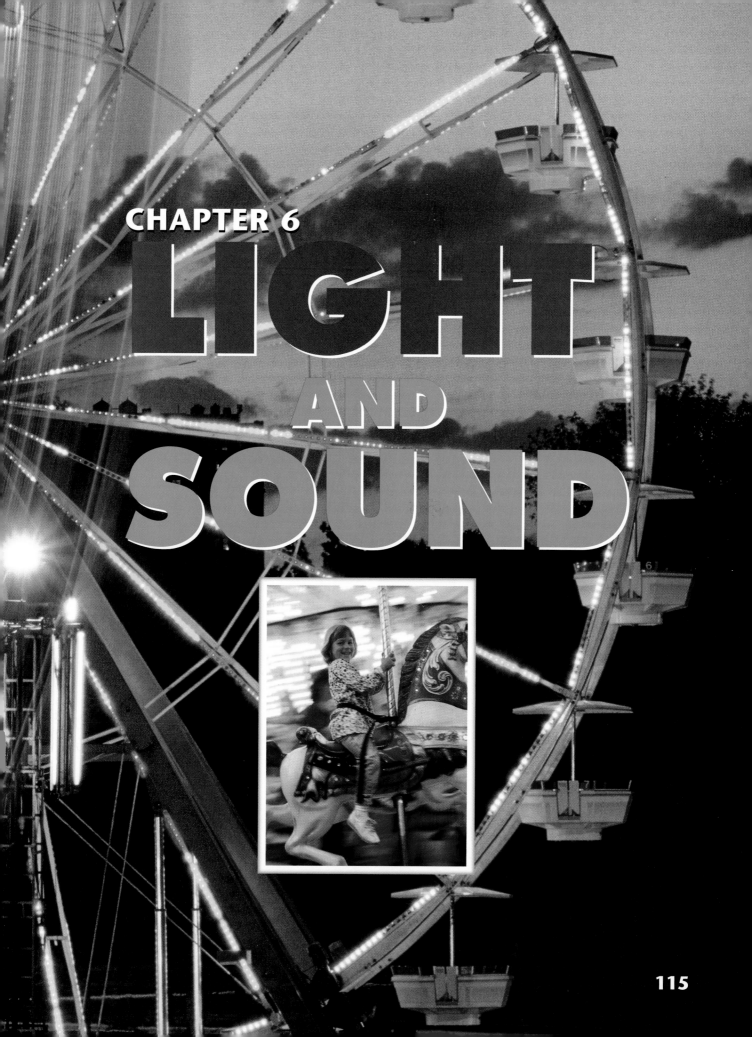

CHAPTER 6
LIGHT
AND
SOUND

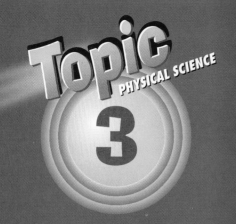

Why it matters

Light can move, but where it moves can be changed.

Science Words

light a kind of energy

reflect bounce off

Light on the Move

What do you see when you look up in the sky? You can see the Sun during the day. What can you see at night?

EXPLORE

Stars shine all the time. So why can't we see all of the stars during the day?

116

Why can't we see all the stars during the day?

What you need

• flashlight

• *Science Journal*

Can you see a flashlight beam during the day? Can you see stars during the day? In this activity you will find out.

What to do

1. **Observe** Make the room dark. Shine a flashlight on the ceiling. Observe.

2. **Observe** Turn on the lights. Observe.

3. **Observe** Go outside. Shine the flashlight on a sunny wall. Observe.

What did you find out?

1. **Identify** When could you best see light from the flashlight? Record in the *Science Journal*.

2. **Identify** When was it hardest to see light from the flashlight? Why?

3. **Infer** Why can't we see all the stars during the day?

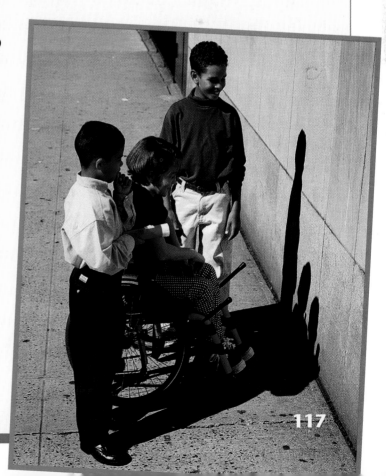

How does light move?

Stars give off light. Light is a kind of energy. The Sun is the closest star to Earth. The Sun's energy gives Earth most of its light and heat.

The Explore Activity shows that light from a flashlight can't be seen on a sunny wall. That's because sunlight is brighter than light from a flashlight. The Sun seems brighter than other stars because it's closer to Earth. This makes it hard to see other stars during the day.

The Sun

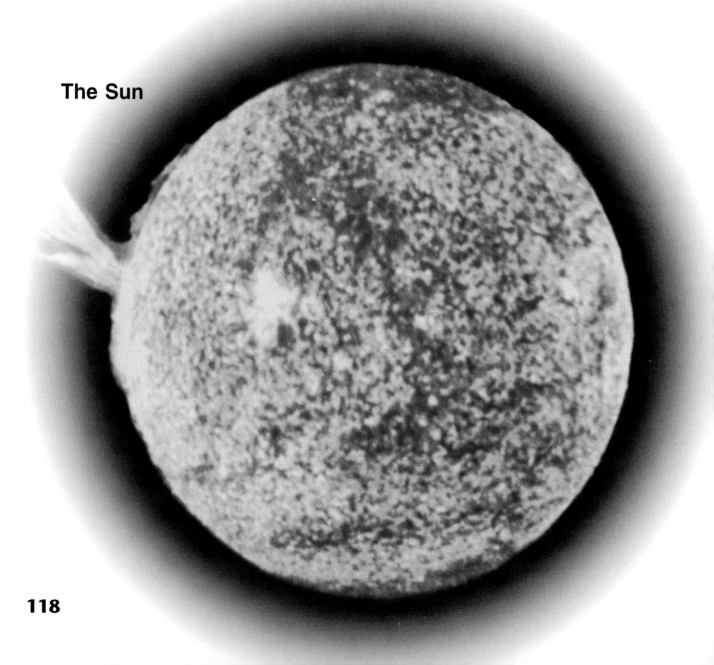

Do you remember that heat moves? Light moves, too. Light moves in a straight path.

Light from the Sun and other stars moves in a straight path to Earth. How does the light from a flashlight move?

How can the path of light be changed?

What happens when you throw a ball against a wall? The ball bounces off the wall. Light can bounce off, or **reflect**, too.

Light reflects off smooth things like mirrors. It reflects off rough things like sidewalks, too. We see things when light reflects off them to our eyes. How has the path of light changed here?

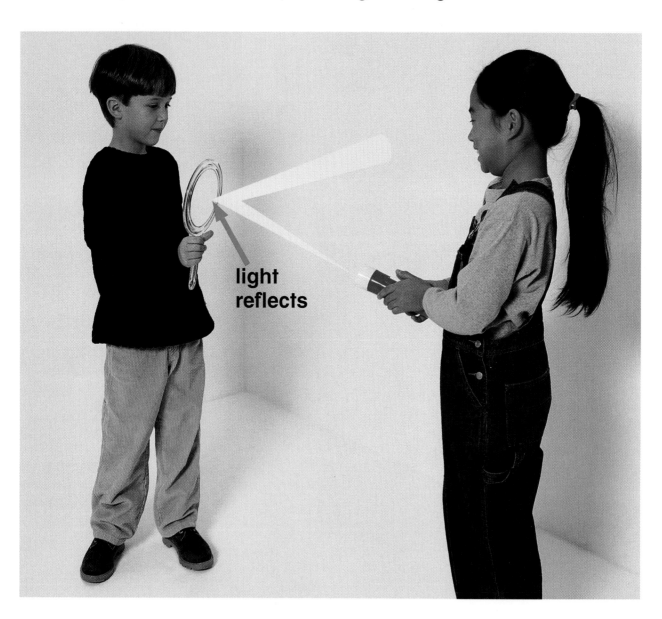

light reflects

Why is light so important to you? You could not see anything without light. Yet sunlight and other bright light can hurt your eyes. How can you keep your eyes safe from very bright light?

REVIEW

1. What is light?

2. From where does Earth get most of its light?

3. How does light move?

4. **Infer** Why can't we see things when it's dark?

5. **Think and Write** How does light move in this picture?

121

Topic
EARTH SCIENCE
4

Why it matters

The stars and Moon seem to change position in the sky over time.

Science Words

constellation a pattern of stars

moon phases the different shapes of the Moon

The Night Sky

When was the last time you looked at the night sky? Did you see stars? Where were the stars? Over your house? Over a tree? Were the stars in the same place when you looked at them later?

EXPLORE

Do the stars move at night? How can you tell?

Does the sky look the same all night?

In this activity you will find out how the night sky changes.

What you need

- *Picture Cards*

- *Science Journal*

What to do

1. **Put in Order** Put the cards in order. How are they the same? How are they different? Record in the *Science Journal*.

2. **Predict** What do you think the next picture will look like?

3. Draw the same picture of your home in each of the 3 boxes in the *Science Journal*.

4. On a clear night, draw the night sky over your home. Record the time. Repeat an hour later and 2 hours later.

What did you find out?

Compare and Contrast What was the same in your drawings? What was different? What does this show?

Does the night sky change?

Have you ever looked at the stars for a long time? The stars seem to make patterns in the sky. A pattern of stars is called a constellation.

There are really many constellations in the night sky. These pictures show only one constellation.

Spring

Summer

The Explore Activity shows that things in the night sky seem to move from hour to hour. How does this constellation seem to move in the sky through the seasons?

Brain Power

Not everyone can see the stars at night. What things might keep us from seeing the stars?

Fall

Winter

Does the Moon change?

The Moon doesn't give off light like the stars. We see the Moon because it reflects light from the Sun.

The Moon seems to change shape, but it doesn't. What changes is how much of the lighted part of the Moon we see.

We see the same pattern of shapes each month. The different shapes of the Moon are called moon phases.

People have always been curious about the Moon and the stars. People write stories and poems about them. People sing about them. People have even been to the Moon. What do you know about the Moon?

REVIEW

1. What things in the night sky seem to change over time?

2. What is a constellation?

3. What about the Moon seems to change?

4. **Infer** Why do people study stars at night?

5. **Think and Write** Do you think that people could live on the Moon? Explain.

127

Why it matters

When something moves, it makes sound, but not all sounds are the same.

Science Words

sound a kind of energy

vibrate move back and forth quickly

pitch how high or how low a sound is

Listen to Sound

Do you have a favorite sound? Is it a whisper? Is it a singing bird? Is it waves on a beach?

Sounds are everywhere. Almost anything can be used to make sound. Have you ever used things to make sounds? What did you do to make the sounds?

EXPLORE

How is sound made? Are all sounds the same?

EXPLORE ACTIVITY

How is sound made?

What happens to strings in 3 different cups when they are snapped?

What you need

- 3 paper cups
- pencil
- 3 pieces of string
- 3 paper clips
- scissors
- goggles
- *Science Journal*

What to do

1. Make a tiny hole in the bottom of the smallest cup. **SAFETY** Wear goggles.

2. Tie string to a paper clip. Pull the string through the hole until the paper clip sits tight in the bottom of the cup.

3. **Observe** You and a partner hold the cup. A third partner snaps the string. Record what happens.

4. Repeat for the other 2 cups.

What did you find out?

1. **Identify** What happens to the string?

2. **Compare and Contrast** How is what happens the same for the 3 cups? How is what happens different for the 3 cups? What makes this difference?

129

What is sound?

The strings in the cup guitar in the Explore Activity make **sound**. Sound is a kind of energy. When something moves back and forth quickly, it **vibrates**. When something vibrates, it makes sound. What vibrates here?

strings vibrate

The sounds made by the cup guitars in the Explore Activity were different. Some sounds were high. Some sounds were low.

Pitch is how high or how low a sound is. Which of these things has a high pitch? Which one has a low pitch?

131

How else can sounds be different?

You know that sounds can be high or low. Sounds can also be loud or soft. All these things make sound. How would you describe these sounds?

132

You hear music. You sing. What are some other things you do that need sound?

REVIEW

1. What is sound?

2. When is a sound made?

3. In what ways can sounds be different?

4. **Identify** Which is louder, someone singing or 4 drums beating? Explain.

5. **Think and Write** Make a list of all the sounds you hear for the next few minutes. Write a word to describe each sound.

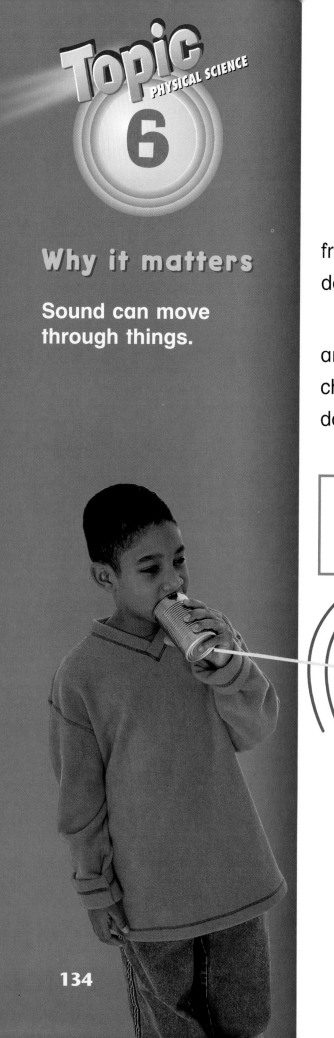

Topic
PHYSICAL SCIENCE
6

Why it matters

Sound can move
through things.

Sound on the Move

How can you talk to your best
friend when you are apart? Can you
do it with string? Yes!

Look at this picture. These children
are far away from each other, yet one
child can hear the other talking. How
does this happen?

EXPLORE

**Can sound move through string?
Can it move through other things?**

Where can sound move?

Can sound move through things? Find out.

What you need
- metal hanger
- string
- pencil
- *Science Journal*

What to do

1. **Observe** Have your partner tap a hanger with a pencil. Record what you observe in the *Science Journal*.

2. Tie a piece of string to each corner of the hanger. Wrap the strings around your pointer fingers. Place your fingers in your ears.

3. Have your partner tap the hanger again with the pencil. Record your observations.

What did you find out?

1. **Identify** What did you observe in steps 1 and 3?

2. **Infer** Where did sound move?

Can sound move through things?

A car horn blows. You hear its sound. How does the sound get from the car horn to you?

READING LINK

1 **Vibrations of the car horn make sound.**

2 **Sound can move through matter, such as solids, liquids, and gases. Here sound moves through air, a gas.**

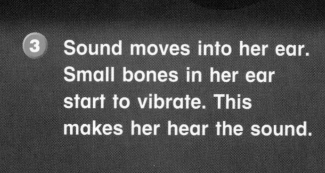

3 **Sound moves into her ear. Small bones in her ear start to vibrate. This makes her hear the sound.**

The Explore Activity shows that sound can move through air. It shows that sound can move through a coat hanger and string, too. Do you think sound can move through your desk? Try it.

Sound moves through solids, like string and your desk, to small bones inside your ear. Then you hear the sounds.

Brain Power

Woodpeckers eat bugs that live under the bark of trees. How do woodpeckers know that bugs are there if they can't see them?

TAP

TAP

TAP

TAP

TAP

TAP

Can sound move through water?

Think about the last time you went swimming. Did you hear anything under the water?

Liquids are another kind of matter. Sound can move through liquids, too.

Very loud sounds move through the air to your ears. These sounds can hurt your ears. What can you do to keep your hearing safe?

REVIEW

1. How do we hear?

2. If you can't see a parade, how can you tell if one is nearby?

3. Someone knocks on a door. Where does the sound move?

4. **Infer** You visit a pet shop. A sign reads "Please don't tap on fish tanks." Why?

5. **Think and Write** What are some very loud sounds that may hurt your ears?

Underwater TALK

Do you ever talk to friends as you swim underwater? You can hear underwater. So can whales and dolphins. In the deep ocean, it's too dark to see far away. Whales and dolphins use sound to find out what's around them.

Life Science Link

The animals make clicking sounds. Then they listen. The clicks bounce back, or reflect, off anything in their way. It might be another whale or dolphin. Or it might be lunch!

Most whales and dolphins live in groups. They "talk" by calling out. The call of some whales sounds like a howling wolf. Other whales whistle. Dolphins whistle and squeal.

Scientists try to copy the whale and dolphin sounds. Someday scientists may be able to talk back to the animals!

DISCUSS

1. What two kinds of sounds do whales and dolphins make?

2. Why do whales and dolphins need good hearing?

Use Science Words

Match each word with its meaning.

1. reflect	a.	how high or low a sound is page 131
2. constellation	b.	quick back and forth movement page 130
3. pitch	c.	bounce page 120
4. sound	d.	a pattern of stars page 124
5. vibrate	e.	a kind of energy page 130

Use Science Ideas

6. How does light move? page 119

7. What are moon phases? page 126

8. Where can sound move? pages 136–138

9. Name something that makes a loud sound. page 132

10. **Contrast** In what way is the Moon different from stars? page 126

PROBLEMS and PUZZLES

Noise Maker Place your hand lightly on your throat and speak. What do you feel? Press your fingers in and out softly while humming. What happens to the sound?

Use Science Words

| constellation | light | reflect | temperature | fuels |

1. A thermometer measures __?__.

2. The energy that stars give off is __?__.

3. We see things because they __?__ light.

4. A pattern of stars is a __?__.

5. Wood and oil are __?__.

Use Ideas and Skills

6. You put a lid on a hot pan. Soon the lid is hot, too. What happened?

7. What happens when a drum vibrates?

8. Name 2 things in the night sky that seem to change.

9. A baby in another room cries. Why do you hear it?

10. **Infer** Why is it usually warmer during the day than at night?

Write in Your Journal

What do you see?
Write about it.

PROBLEMS and PUZZLES

Heat Moves

If a hot object touches a cold object, which way will heat move? The arrow shows where heat moves in the first pair of objects. Copy the other pairs of objects. Draw arrows to show which way heat will move. Use the temperature key to help you.

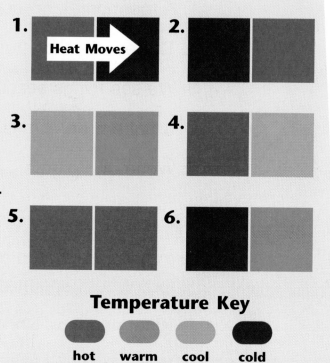

Temperature Key

hot   warm   cool   cold

Mirror, Mirror

Write a word on a piece of paper. Reflect the word in a mirror. The letters are backward! How can you make the letters read correctly again? Think of a way.

CHAPTER 7

FORCES AND MACHINES

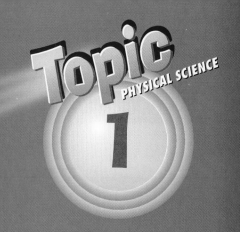

Topic
PHYSICAL SCIENCE
1

Why it matters

Heavy things need bigger pushes or pulls to move than lighter things.

Science Words

force a push or a pull

gravity a force that pulls between things and Earth

Pushes and Pulls, Big and Small

How do you know that something has moved? You know when you see that something is in a different place than it was before.

The children move up. Then they move down. Their position changes.

EXPLORE

What makes things move? Do all objects move the same way?

How can we make things move?

You will observe how different things move when you move them the same way.

What you need

- paper
- checker
- wood block
- *Science Journal*

What to do

1. Crumple paper. Line up the paper, block, and checker along a desk.

2. **Predict** Which thing will move farthest if you move each one the same way? Record in the *Science Journal*.

3. Try to move each thing. Be sure not to move one thing harder than the other. Record what happens.

What did you find out?

1. **Identify** How did you move each thing?

2. **Infer** Which thing moved farthest in step 3? Why do you think this happened?

147

What are forces?

The Explore Activity shows that things like blocks, paper, and checkers cannot move on their own. It takes a push or a pull to move things. A push or a pull is a force.

How does the girl close the door? She pushes it. A push is a force. How does the girl move the sled? She pulls it. A pull is a force, too.

pull

push

What happens when you jump up? Something pulls you back down. Something pulls the ball back down, too. That something is a force called **gravity**. Gravity is a force that pulls between things and Earth.

Gravity pulls more on heavy things than on light things. Which do you think gravity pulls on more, a 10-pound bowling ball or an 8-pound bowling ball? Why?

How do we use numbers?

You didn't have to pick up a 10-pound bowling ball to know that it was heavier than an 8-pound bowling ball, did you? That's because numbers can tell you about things.

Numbers help you count and measure. Numbers tell you how many or how much. Numbers help you know how things are alike and different without even seeing them.

SKILL BUILDER

Use Numbers

How much force does it take to move different objects? Use numbers to compare.

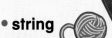

What you need

- scissors
- cardboard
- string
- thin rubber band
- paper clip
- bottle of glue
- tape
- goggles
- *Science Journal*

What to do

1. Have your teacher help you make the Puller Pal. **SAFETY** Wear goggles.

2. Tie scissors to the end of the string. Pull the scissors along your desk slowly with the Puller Pal.

3. **Use Numbers** As you pull, your partner reads the number that the rubber band stretches to. Write it in the *Science Journal*.

4. Repeat using the bottle of glue.

What did you find out?

1. **Compare** Which thing showed the larger number when pulled?

2. **Infer** Which thing took more pulling force to move?

151

How much force is needed to move things?

The boy cannot move the desk by himself. He cannot push hard enough. Yet when a friend helps, the desk moves. Why? Two people can make a stronger pushing force than one person.

When the boy empties the desk, he can move it by himself. Why?

Knowing about forces and how things move can help you get a job done.

The boy could not move the heavy desk by himself before. Now he can. Why?

REVIEW

1. What is a force?

2. What makes things move?

3. What is gravity?

4. **Use Numbers** One box is 35 pounds. Another box is 40 pounds. Which box is heavier? How do you know?

5. **Think and Write** A wagon with toys is too heavy to move. How can you move the wagon? Use the word *force* in your answer.

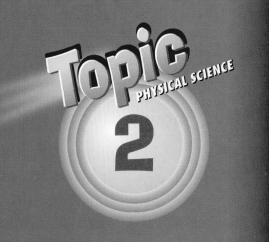

Why it matters

Forces change the way things move.

Science Words

friction the rubbing of one thing on another

Forces and Change

Did you ever roll a ball to others?
These children are doing just that!

EXPLORE

How does force change the way things move?

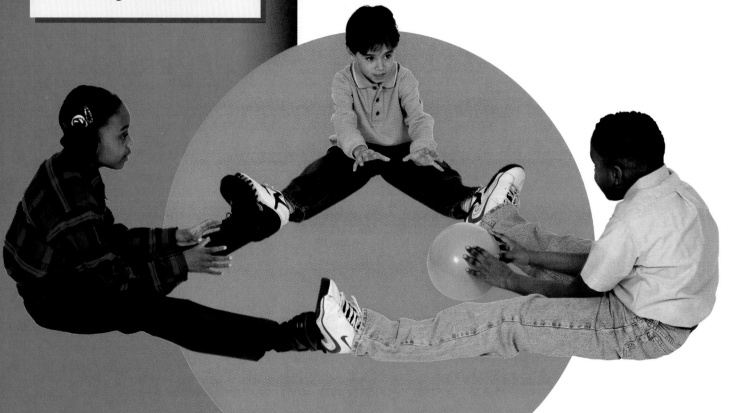

How many ways can a ball move?

How can force change the way a ball moves? Let's find out.

What you need
- rubber ball
- *Science Journal*

What to do

1. Play a game. Sit on the floor with some partners, like this.

2. Take turns rolling a ball back and forth.

3. Make the ball go faster, then slower.

4. Make the ball go in different directions.

What did you find out?

1. **Explain** What did you do to make the ball go faster? Slower? Record in the *Science Journal*.

2. **Explain** What did you do to make the ball move in a different direction?

How do forces change the way things move?

The Explore Activity shows that when a force changes, the way a thing moves changes, too. Look at how the pulling force changes here. Each change in force makes the wagon move differently.

1 A pulling force starts the wagon moving.

2 When the pulling force gets stronger, the wagon moves faster.

3 One girl leaves. The pulling force gets weaker. The wagon slows down.

4 The direction of the force changes. It makes the wagon's direction change.

5 The girl stops pulling. The wagon's wheels rub against the floor until the wagon stops.

What slows things down?

These wheels rub against the ground. This rubbing makes the wagon and skates slow down. The rubbing of one thing on another is called **friction** (FRIK shuhn).

NATIONAL GEOGRAPHIC

FUNtastic Facts

Friction makes planes slow down and stop. What parts are rubbing? What else can friction do? Try rubbing your hands. What do you feel? What happens to the wheels of the plane?

You know how to use force to start your bike moving. You also know how to change the force to slow down and stop your bike. Which child uses more force here? Why?

REVIEW

1. What happens to a moving thing when it is pulled or pushed harder?

2. Two children push a box. One child stops pushing. How does the box move now?

3. What happens to a moving thing when the direction of its force changes?

4. **Infer** Why do some shoes have bumps on the bottom?

5. **Think and Write** What will happen if you give a quick push to an empty box on the floor?

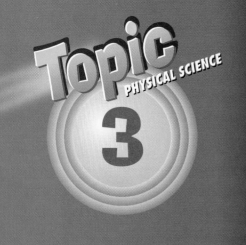

Why it matters

Levers can be used to help lift things.

Science Words

simple machine anything that can change the direction and size of forces

lever a simple machine used to change the force needed to lift things

fulcrum the point that holds up the bar of a lever

Levers

Each time, the child tries to lift the book with a pencil. Each time, the bottom pencil is at a different distance from the book. Describe where the bottom pencil is in each picture.

EXPLORE

Where will it be easiest to lift the book using the pencil? Where will it be hardest to lift the book using the pencil?

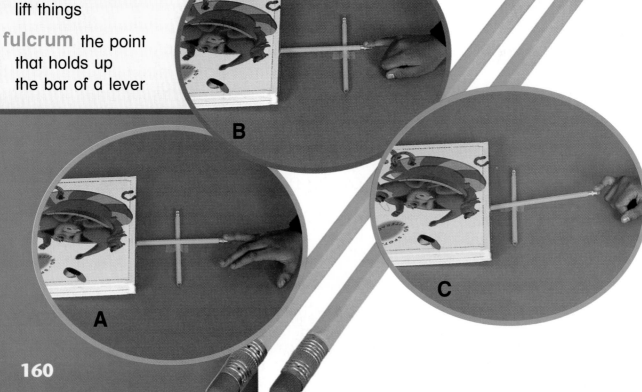

B

A

C

What is the easiest way to lift a book?

What you need

- 2 unsharpened pencils
- heavy book
- tape
- *Science Journal*

In this activity you will find out the best place to put a pencil to lift a heavy book.

What to do

1. **Predict** Look at page 160. Which way would be easiest to lift a heavy book? Record in the *Science Journal*.

2. Tape a pencil to your desk. Place the book and other pencil as shown in pictures A–C on page 160.

3. Each time, push down on the end of the pencil with your smallest finger. Record what happens.

What did you find out?

1. **Compare** When was it hardest to lift the book? When was it easiest to lift the book?

2. **Infer** What made the difference?

How does a lever work?

A lot of force is needed to lift heavy things. The Explore Activity shows how a **simple machine** is used to lift a heavy book. A simple machine is anything that can change the direction and size of forces. The simple machine used here is a **lever** (LEV ur). A lever is a simple machine that may be used to change the force needed to lift things. A lever has a hard bar and a point that holds up the bar. The point that holds up the bar of a lever is called the **fulcrum**.

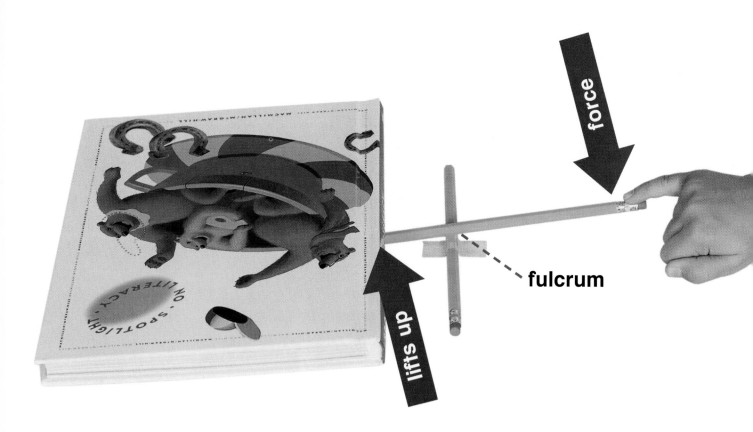

force

lifts up

fulcrum

Have you ever been on a seesaw with someone who is about your weight? Did you know that a seesaw is a lever?

To make the seesaw work, one boy pushes against the ground with his feet and legs. This force lifts him up and makes the other side of the seesaw come down. Where on this seesaw is the fulcrum?

force

lifts up

fulcrum

Where do we use levers?

All of these simple machines are levers. What are these levers called? How does each one work?

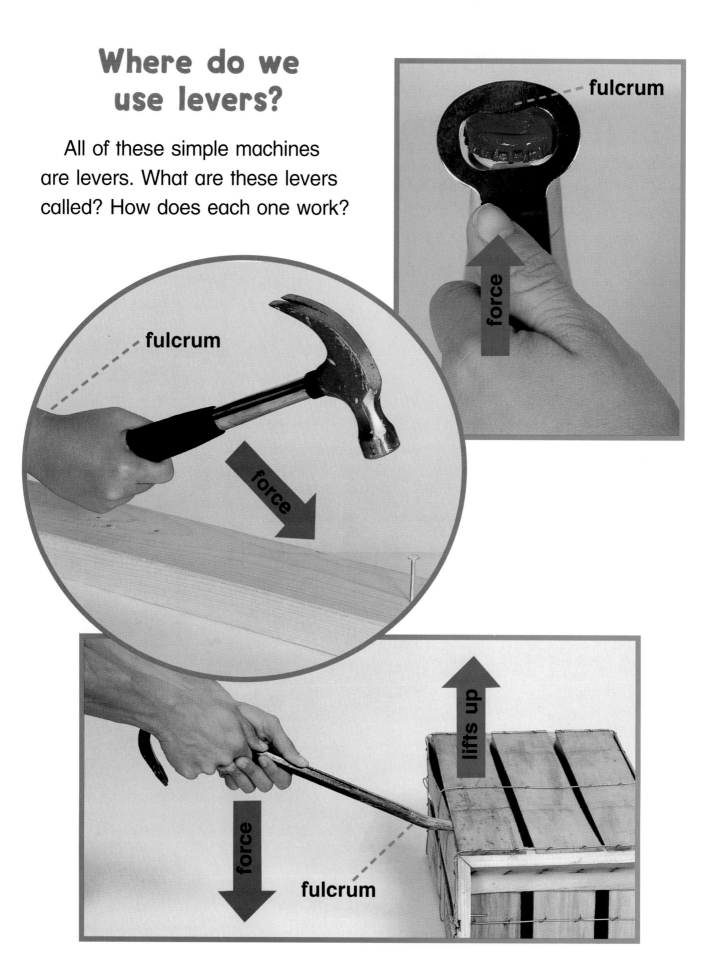

fulcrum

force

fulcrum

force

lifts up

force

fulcrum

Levers help make your work easier. They also help you have fun. What do these levers help you do?

1. What is a simple machine?

2. What is a lever?

3. Name the parts of a lever.

4. **Communicate** Name a lever and tell how it works.

5. **Think and Write** You try but cannot move a heavy rock with a lever. What could you do to move the rock?

Why it matters

Ramps can be used to help lift things.

Science Words

ramp a simple machine with a slanted surface

Ramps

How can you get the elephant onto the truck? You couldn't lift it, could you? An elephant is much too heavy to lift. Is there an easier way to do this?

EXPLORE

How can you move heavy things without lifting them straight up?

Which way is easier?

Is it easier to pull something up a board or lift it straight up? Find out.

What you need
- washers
- Puller Pal
- goggles
- books
- 2-foot cardboard
- *Science Journal*

What to do

1. Tie 10 washers onto the end of the Puller Pal from page 151.
   SAFETY Wear goggles.

2. **Use Numbers** Lift the washers. Find and record the number shown on the Puller Pal in the *Science Journal*.

3. Place a board on some books like this. Pull the washers up the board slowly.

4. **Use Numbers** Find and record the number shown on the Puller Pal.

What did you find out?

Compare When was it easier to move the washers? Why do you say so?

How does a ramp work?

Did you ever try to lift something very heavy? You know that lifting heavy things takes a lot of force.

This man has a tough job to do. How could he make the job easier?

The man can use a **ramp**. A ramp is a simple machine with a slanted surface. The Explore Activity shows how a ramp lets you move things with less force than lifting.

A ramp can be short and steep. It can also be long and not as steep. It takes more force to push something up a steep ramp than one that is not as steep. What kind of ramp would let the man use even less force?

Where do we use ramps?

Where are ramps used here? How are the ramps in these pictures different? How are they the same?

You see and use ramps every day and may not even know it! These simple machines help you get where you are going. What ramps did you use today?

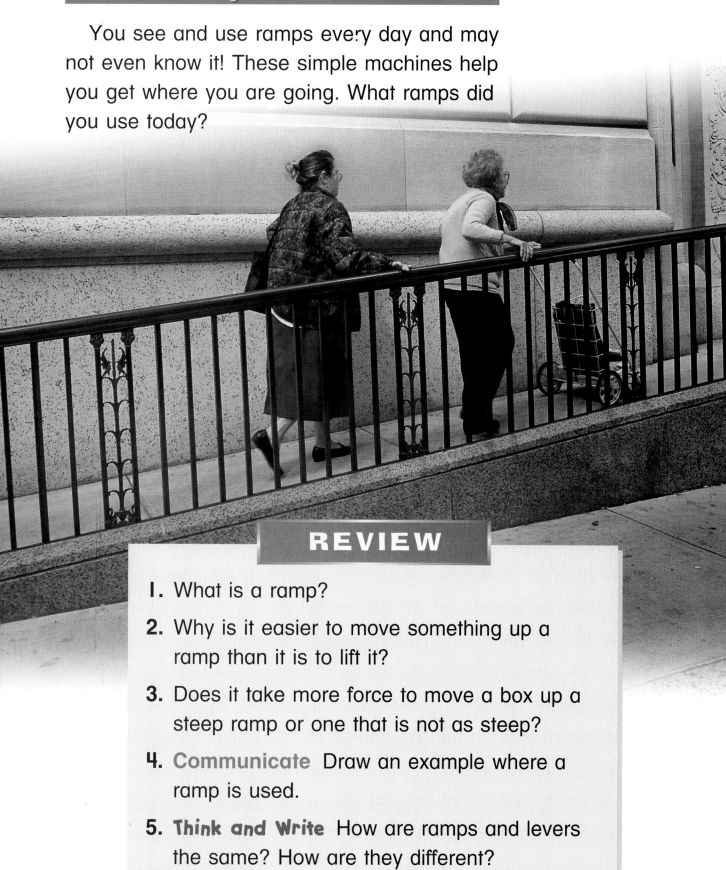

REVIEW

1. What is a ramp?

2. Why is it easier to move something up a ramp than it is to lift it?

3. Does it take more force to move a box up a steep ramp or one that is not as steep?

4. **Communicate** Draw an example where a ramp is used.

5. **Think and Write** How are ramps and levers the same? How are they different?

171

Living Levers!

Did you know that you use levers to move your body? Your bones act as levers. Your muscles move those levers. Your joints, the places where bones meet, act as fulcrums.

Health Link

When you pick up a ball, you use a lever. The muscles in your upper arm pull the bones in your lower arm and lift the ball. The elbow joint is the fulcrum.

When you stand on your tiptoes, you use other levers. The muscles in the back of your lower legs pull, or lift, your heels.

Discuss

1 Which parts of your body act like levers?

2 Which parts of your body act like fulcrums?

Use Science Words

fulcrum
gravity
ramp
lever
friction
force

1. A push or pull is a ___?___. page 148

2. Rubbing that slows things is ___?___. page 158

3. The force that pulls on you is ___?___. page 149

4. A slanted surface is a ___?___. page 169

5. The point that holds up the bar of a lever is the ___?___. page 162

6. A simple machine that changes the force needed to lift things is a ___?___ page 162

Use Science Ideas

7. Where does gravity pull more—on a pencil, or on a book? Why? page 149

8. What happens when you push a moving thing harder? pages 156–157

9. Which would you use to lift a heavy box onto a truck—a lever, or a ramp? pages 162, 169

10. **Use Numbers** Is it harder to push the same box up a 6-foot ramp, or a 9-foot ramp? Why? pages 150–151, 169

PROBLEMS and PUZZLES

Rise and Shine Invent a machine to get your older brother or sister out of bed. Use levers and ramps. Draw a picture of your machine.

CHAPTER 8
FORCES AND MAGNETS

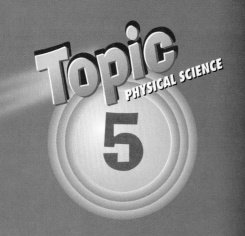

Why it matters

Magnets can pull some kinds of things.

Science Words

attract pull

poles the places on a magnet where its pull is strongest

repel push away

All About Magnets

Have you ever held a magnet? The pictures show what happens when you move a magnet close to paper clips.

EXPLORE

Does this happen to all things that a magnet comes close to?

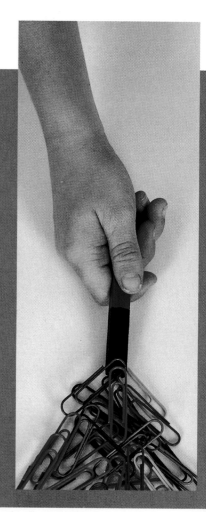

What will stick to a magnet?

What kind of objects will stick to a magnet? Find out.

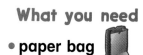

What you need

- paper bag
- metal objects
- nonmetal objects
- ring magnet
- string
- pencil
- *Science Journal*

What to do

1. Work with 2 partners. Make a fishing pole like this one. Put all the objects in a lunch bag.

2. **Predict** What kind of fish will you catch? Record in the *Science Journal*.

3. Take turns fishing until nothing comes out of the bag. Put your catch in a pile.

4. Put the things left in the bag in another pile.

What did you find out?

1. **Compare** How are the things you caught the same?

2. **Infer** What things will stick to a magnet?

177

When do magnets pull?

The Explore Activity shows that some things can stick to a magnet. Magnets pull, or attract, some kinds of things. Magnets attract things made of iron. Yet magnets do not attract all metal things. A magnet will not attract a copper penny or a brass tack.

A magnet also does not attract things made of wood or glass. Why does the magnet attract these things?

Magnets have two **poles**. The poles are the places where a magnet's pull is strongest. One pole is called the North pole, or N pole. The other pole is called the South pole, or S pole. The poles are at the ends on a bar magnet.

Magnets can also attract other magnets. Which poles of the magnets here attract each other?

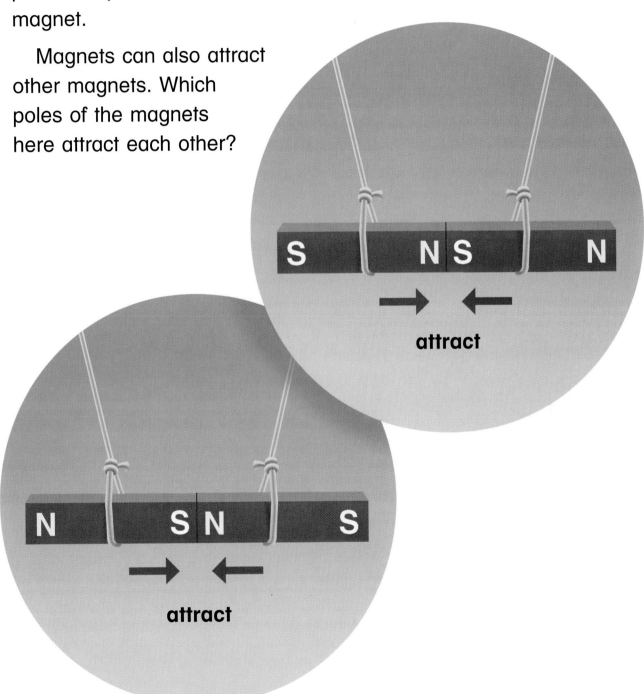

attract

attract

When do magnets push?

Magnets attract each other when different poles come near. Look at what happens when the N poles of these magnets come near. Look at what happens when the S poles of these magnets come near.

These magnets did not attract, did they? Poles that are the same repel each other. Poles that repel push each other away.

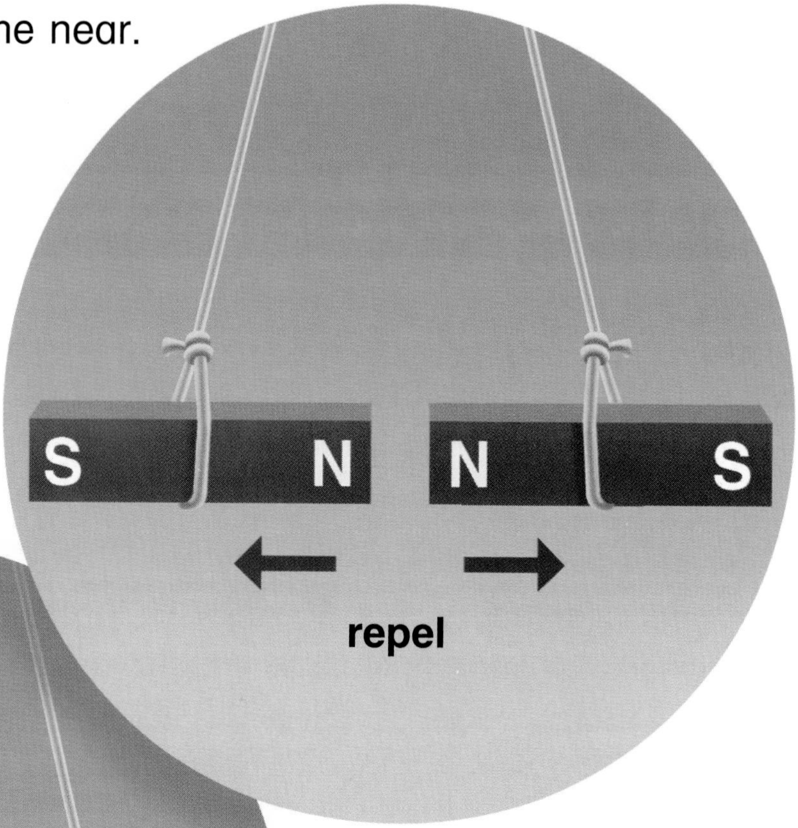

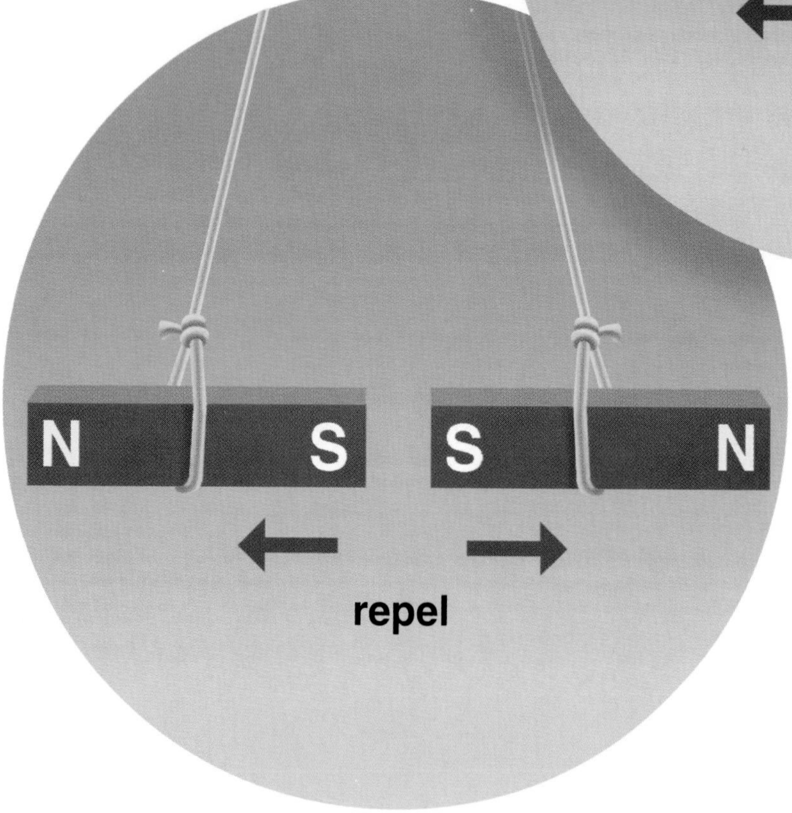

repel

repel

The push and pull of magnets can do things for you. You probably have magnets in your home. How are magnets used here?

REVIEW

1. What do magnets attract?

2. What happens when N comes near S on two magnets?

3. What happens when S comes near S on two magnets?

4. **Infer** What is the pole on the unmarked magnet? How do you know?

5. **Think and Write** List the places where magnets are used in your classroom.

Topic 6
PHYSICAL SCIENCE

Why it matters

Magnets can pull through things.

Science Words

magnetic field the place around a magnet where its force pulls or pushes

A Magnet's Force

Did you ever see a paper clip do this? You might think that this happens by magic, but it does not. Magnets have a space around them that attracts some objects.

EXPLORE

How big is the space around a magnet that can pull things to it?

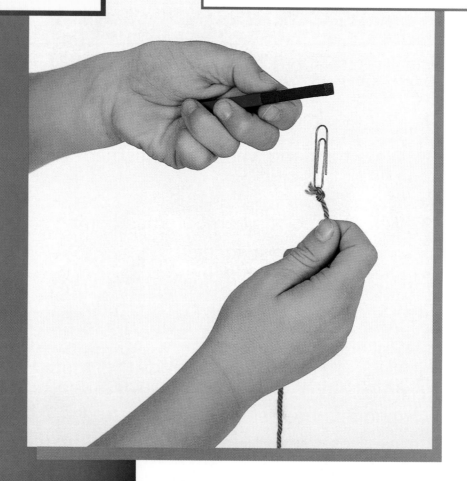

Where is a magnet's pulling space?

Observe a magnet's pulling space. Can the pulling force pass through things?

What you need

- bar magnet
- string
- paper clip
- index card
- *Science Journal*

What to do

1. **Observe** Tie a clip to a string. Pass the clip back and forth slowly over a magnet. Come only as close as you must to feel the magnet's pull.

2. **Communicate** Draw the space where the magnet pulls in the *Science Journal*.

3. **Observe** Place an index card on the magnet. Pass the clip over the magnet again.

What did you find out?

1. **Explain** Tell about the space where the magnet pulls in step 1.

2. **Infer** What happens in step 3? Why?

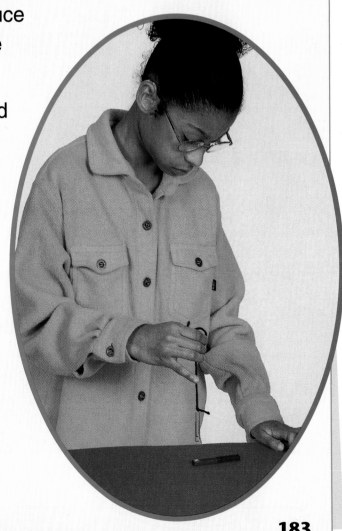

What can magnets pull through?

Did you ever play with a game like this? Tiny pieces of iron are inside. You move them to draw a picture. How does the girl make the clown's hair?

The Explore Activity shows that a magnet has a certain space where a paper clip can be pulled to it. The paper clip cannot be pulled to the magnet outside this space.

A magnet's pull or push is called its force. This force is strong enough to pull or push through many kinds of things. In the Explore Activity, the magnet's force pulls the paper clip through the index card. Through what does this magnet pull?

What is a magnetic field?

Suppose you place tiny pieces of iron inside a jar of baby oil. What happens if you put a magnet into the jar? The force of the magnet moves the iron pieces. You see a magnetic field (mag NET ik feeld) around the magnet. The magnetic field is the place around a magnet where its force pulls or pushes.

Brain Power

Where in the magnetic field are the most pieces of iron found? Why do you think this is?

Earth is like a big magnet. It has a huge magnetic field that stretches out into space. Where is the force of Earth's magnet strongest?

REVIEW

1. Name some things through which a magnet can pull.

2. What is the push or pull of a magnet called?

3. What is a magnetic field?

4. **Communicate** Draw a magnetic field around a bar magnet.

5. **Think and Write** Suppose you drop a nail in a bucket of water. How can you get the nail out and keep your hands dry?

Riding a

Japan's bullet train doesn't run on a track. It floats 15 centimeters (6 inches) above a rail!

The rail has magnets in it. So does the bottom of the train. The like poles of the magnets push away from each other. This makes the train float. The ride is very smooth and quiet.

Electricity in the track creates a wave of energy. It pushes the train forward.

This train goes faster than other trains. It uses less fuel, too. That means it pollutes less!

Some places in the United States plan to have trains like this. Maybe someday you'll ride a wave of energy!

WAVE

DISCUSS

1. How do magnets make the bullet train float?

2. How is the bullet train different from other trains?

Use Science Words

attract

poles

repel

magnetic field

1. Magnets that push away from each other ____?____. page 180

2. Magnets pull or ____?____. page 178

3. A magnet is strongest at its ____?____. page 179

4. The place around a magnet where its force pulls or pushes is its ____?____. page 186

Use Science Ideas

5. What does a magnet attract? page 178

6. Name a magnet's poles. page 179

7. When 2 magnets come close, which poles attract? page 179

8. When 2 magnets come close, which poles repel? p.180

9. Name 2 things a magnet can pull through. p.185

10. **Infer** Which magnet is stronger? How can you tell?

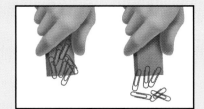

PROBLEMS and PUZZLES

North Pole Make a compass like this one. Rub a needle on a bar magnet 50 times in the same direction. Tape the needle to a cork. Put it in water. Can you find north?

UNIT 4 REVIEW

Use Science Words

force	friction	lever	ramp	repel

1. The N poles of 2 magnets __?__.

2. The rubbing that slows a moving bicycle is __?__.

3. A slanted surface makes a __?__.

4. When you pull, you use __?__.

5. A seesaw is a kind of __?__.

Use Ideas and Skills

6. You jump up. What happens? Why?

7. A girl pushes a box. What happens when the girl stops pushing?

8. Which is easier to use, a steep ramp or one that is not steep?

9. When can a magnet attract a nail?

10.  **Use Numbers** Which is easier to move, a wagon with 20 pounds of dirt, or one with 45 pounds of dirt? Explain.

Write in Your Journal

What do you see? Write about it.

PROBLEMS and PUZZLES

Friction Game

Play with partners. Pick a topic. Then go around the circle. Each player completes a sentence that begins: "Without friction..." The examples shown are for the topic "Circus." Repeat the game for other topics.

Without friction the clown couldn't grip the balls to juggle.

Without friction the seal couldn't hold its ball.

Without friction the tires couldn't grip the road.

Seesaw Problems

Look at each seesaw. Where would you move the post to balance each group of riders? Draw a picture to show it. Then make up your own seesaw problems. Trade them with a friend.

UNIT 5

ROCKY HOMES

CHAPTER 9

AT HOME IN A CANYON

Needs of Living Things

Why it matters

Living things get what they need from the places where they live.

How would you like to live in a place a mile deep? That's how deep the Grand Canyon is in some parts.

A river flows along the bottom of this rocky place. Do you think that anything could live here? Why or why not?

EXPLORE

Is this rocky place a good place for shelter?

Science Words

canyon a deep place with steep hills on either side

classify to group things that are alike in some way

habitat a place where a plant or animal lives

Shelter Among the Rocks

Are outside and inside temperatures the same? Find out in this activity.

What you need

• thermometer

• *Science Journal*

What to do

1. **Measure** Find the temperature inside your classroom. Record it on the bar graph in the *Science Journal.*

   ⚠ **SAFETY** Handle the thermometer carefully.

2. **Measure** Find and record the temperatures of 3 different places in your schoolyard.

What did you find out?

1. **Compare** Were the schoolyard temperatures higher or lower than the classroom temperature?

2. **Infer** What does the classroom shelter you from?

3. **Draw Conclusions** What does a rocky home shelter an animal from?

What do living things need?

rattlesnake

Just like you, animals and plants need air, food, and water. Animals need shelter, too.

The Explore Activity shows that shelter protects animals from hot and cold temperatures. It may protect them from wind, water, and enemies, too. These animals get shelter in a **canyon**. A canyon is a deep place with steep hills on either side.

eagle

Some animals of the canyon eat plants. Some eat other animals. Other animals eat both plants and animals.

Canyon animals get water from rivers and puddles. Some animals get water in other ways. Look at the bird. How does it get water?

cactus wren

puma

How can you classify?

When scientists talk about animals, they often **classify** them. Classify means to group things that are alike in some way. These buttons are classified by their color. Some are red. Some are green. Some are blue.

The buttons may also be classified by shape. Some of the buttons are round. Some are square. Can you think of another way to classify these buttons?

Classify

In this activity you will classify some canyon animals.

What you need

• *Picture Cards*

• *Science Journal*

What to do

1. **Classify** Classify the animals shown on the Picture Cards by their body covering.

2. **Change It** Put the animals together again. Classify them by the number of feet each animal has.

What did you find out?

1. **Identify** How many groups did you have in step 1? Step 2?

2. **Explain** What did you do to classify the animals?

3. **Identify** What is another way to classify these animals?

199

What is a habitat?

A **habitat** is a place where a plant or animal lives. Living things get what they need to live from their habitat. Living things get air, water, a place to live, and food from their habitat. What living things would an animal get from this habitat? What nonliving things would it get?

NATIONAL GEOGRAPHIC

FUNtastic Facts

Some habitats are hot and dry. A desert in Chile, in South America, once had no rain for 14 years! What was it like to live there?

Many people visit canyons. Some people do things that change canyon habitats. Some people pollute the canyon with trash. Some people flying planes can scare away canyon animals. The bridges that people build make canyon walls break apart. What should people do?

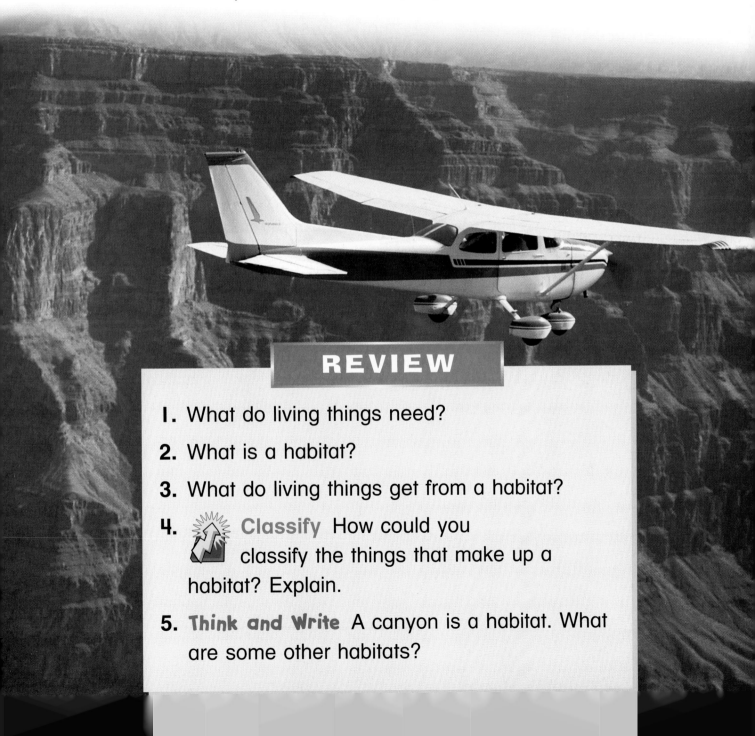

REVIEW

1. What do living things need?

2. What is a habitat?

3. What do living things get from a habitat?

4. **Classify** How could you classify the things that make up a habitat? Explain.

5. **Think and Write** A canyon is a habitat. What are some other habitats?

Why it matters

The body parts of animals help them get food and stay safe.

Science Words

predator an animal that hunts another animal for food

prey animals that are hunted

Living in Rocky Homes

What do you think is about to happen in this picture? Each animal is looking for food. What do you think each animal eats?

Now look at the eyes of each animal. Where are the eyes of each animal?

EXPLORE

How do eyes help an animal find food and stay safe?

EXPLORE ACTIVITY

Why are eyes where they are?

This activity will show you how different animals use their eyes.

What you need

• 2 paper tubes

• *Science Journal*

What to do

1. Stand in front of a partner. Look through the paper tubes.

2. **Observe** Your partner will move his or her arms forward. Tell when you first see their fingers.

3. **Change It** Try again without the paper tubes. Now let your partner try. Talk about what you notice. Write it in the *Science Journal*.

What did you find out?

1. **Identify** When did you see fingers coming from behind?

2. **Infer** Suppose you were a deer. What kind of eyes would you want — eyes that saw straight ahead, or to the sides? Why?

Why can animals live in rocky homes?

Animals have special body parts to help them find food or stay safe.

The Explore Activity shows why the eyes of animals are different. The puma's eyes are in the front of its head. They help the puma see what it hunts. Where are the eyes of the sheep? How does this help the sheep?

The sheep's hooves help it to run on rocks. It can get away from enemies and find food.

puma

bighorn sheep

Look at the snake's tail. The tail looks and sounds like a rattle. The snake shakes its rattle to warn away its enemies.

The eagle has special claws. It can grab the snake and fly away with it in these claws.

Brain Power

Look at the eagle's beak. Why do you think that the beak is shaped this way?

eagle

rattlesnake

What do they eat?

An animal that hunts another animal for food is called a **predator**. The puma hunts the sheep. The puma is a predator.

Animals that are hunted are called **prey**. The sheep is the prey.

Look at the eagle and the snake. Which is the predator? Which is the prey?

206

The living things in a habitat need each other. Some snakes eat mice for food. Do mice need snakes?

If snakes did not eat mice, there would be too many of them. There would not be enough food for all the mice. Then what would happen to mice?

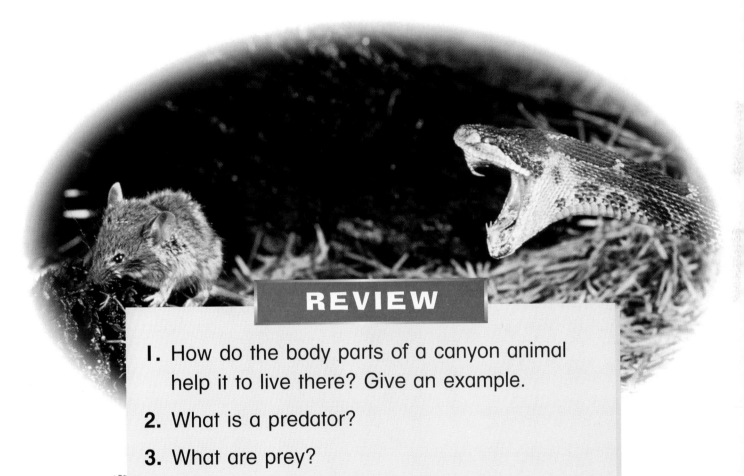

REVIEW

1. How do the body parts of a canyon animal help it to live there? Give an example.

2. What is a predator?

3. What are prey?

4. **Communicate** Draw a picture of a predator and its prey.

5. **Think and Write** Some predators are also prey. Give an example.

Why it matters

All animals grow up to look like their parents, but they don't all have the same life cycles.

Science Words

pupa the stage before the adult butterfly

Animal Life Cycles

Did you ever see such cute puppies? In what ways do the puppies look like their mother and each other? In what ways do they look different from their mother and each other?

EXPLORE

How can animals that belong to the same group be different?

Alike, Yet Different

You will tell how animals are alike and different.

What you need

- Picture Cards
- Science Journal

What to do

1. **Classify** Work with a partner. Choose a *Picture Card*. Find other animals that are like the one you chose. Put them into a group.

2. Make 2 more groups. Put animals that are alike into their own group.

What did you find out?

1. **Compare** How are the animals in each group the same? Write about each group in the *Science Journal*.

2. **Contrast** How are the animals in each group different? Write about each group.

How do young animals grow?

You can tell dogs, snakes, and butterflies apart. All dogs are like other dogs in many ways. All snakes are like other snakes in many ways. All butterflies are like other butterflies in many ways. Yet each dog looks different from other dogs. Each snake and butterfly looks different from other snakes and butterflies, too. The Explore Activity shows this.

Animals look different from each other, but animals are also alike. How? All animals grow up to look like their parents. Young mice grow up to be adult mice. Mice never grow up to be frogs.

There is another way that animals are alike. All animals have a life cycle. A life cycle begins when an animal is born or is hatched. It grows up to be an adult. The adult has young that look like itself. The life cycle ends when the animal dies.

Life Cycle of a Kangaroo Rat

just born

young animal

adult animal

How do butterflies grow?

Not all animals have the same life cycle. When a butterfly lays an egg, the young that hatches does not look at all like the parent. Instead, the young animal looks like a worm called a caterpillar (KAT ur pihl ur).

The caterpillar turns into a pupa (PYOO puh). A pupa is the stage before the adult butterfly. After a few weeks, the pupa turns into an adult butterfly.

Life Cycle of a Butterfly

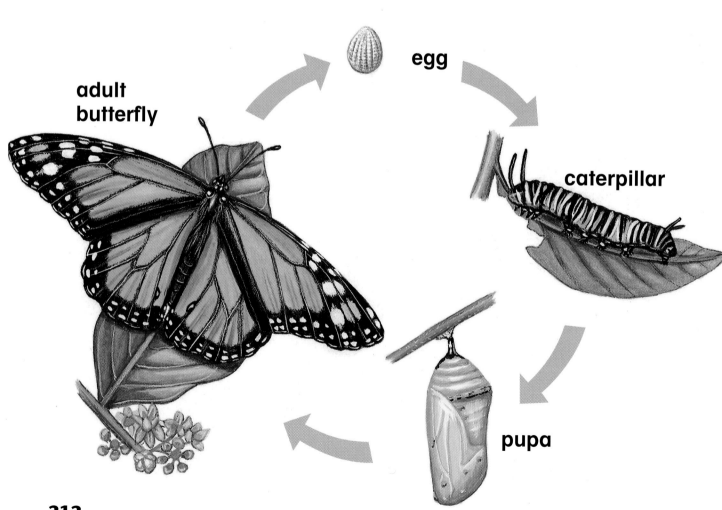

egg

adult butterfly

caterpillar

pupa

Like other animals, you will grow to look like your parents. Yet you will not look exactly like your parents.

Like other animals, you have a life cycle, too. You were born. You will grow to be an adult. Someday you may have children that will look like you.

1. How are dogs alike? How are they different?

2. How are the life cycles of animals the same?

3. What is a pupa?

4. **Communicate** How is the life cycle of a butterfly different from the life cycle of a mouse? Explain.

5. **Think and Write** Draw what you think the life cycle of an eagle would look like.

213

Protecting Peregrines

This peregrine falcon lives on a high, rocky cliff. Not too long ago, only a few peregrines were left in this country. They were almost extinct.

A Closer Look

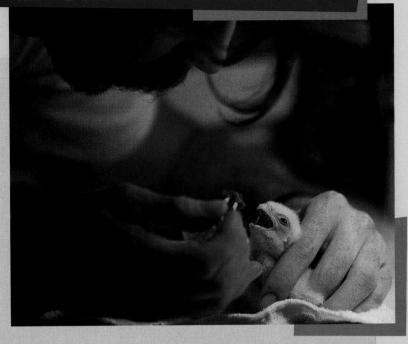

Scientists studied the problem. They started raising baby peregrines. When the chicks were old enough, scientists returned some to rocky cliffs. They released others in cities. The peregrines began to raise chicks of their own.

Now there are plenty of peregrines again. In the city, peregrines nest on the ledges of tall buildings. This one has a nest on the 39th floor!

Discuss

1 How did scientists protect the peregrine?

2 What other animals are almost extinct?

Use Science Words

| prey |
| classify |
| habitat |
| canyon |
| predators |
| pupa |

1. Animals hunted for food are ___?___. page 206

2. A deep place with hills on either side is a ___?___. page 196

3. A place where plants and animals live is a ___?___. page 200

4. Animals that hunt other animals are ___?___. page 206

5. To group things that are alike in some way means to ___?___. page 198

6. The stage before the adult butterfly is the ___?___. page 212

Use Science Ideas

7. What do living things get from their habitat? page 200

8. How do hooves help a sheep live? page 204

9. How are animal life cycles the same? page 212

10. **Classify** How you would classify a mouse, a snake, and a puma? page 199

PROBLEMS and PUZZLES

Snug as a bug Think of a small animal, like a bug or fish. What would you need to make a habitat for it? How could you give the animal what it needed?

CHAPTER 10
MAKING A HOME IN THE CANYON

Why it matters

Rocks are different in many ways, and can be used by people.

Science Words

properties how a thing looks, feels, smells, tastes, or sounds

Properties of Rocks

Have you ever really looked at a rock? Rocks are everywhere. You walk on them. You see them all over the ground. You see them in the walls of buildings and on the sides of canyon trails.

EXPLORE

There are many kinds of rocks. What are some ways that rocks can be different from each other?

EXPLORE ACTIVITY

How can you classify rocks?

In this activity you will classify rocks.

What to do

1. **Observe** Observe your rock with a hand lens. Write words that tell about your rock in the *Science Journal.*

2. **Classify** Work with 4 other children. Make 2 circles with the yarn. Each of you takes a turn. Classify the rocks into 2 groups. Let others guess the rule used to classify.

SAFETY Wash your hands when you finish the activity.

What did you find out?

1. **Identify** Which senses did you use to classify rocks?

2. **Communicate** What rules did your group use?

What you need

- small rock
- hand lens
- 2 long pieces of yarn
- *Science Journal*

219

What are some properties of rocks?

Here is how two children classified their rocks from the Explore Activity. Rosa classified the rocks by light color and dark color. Beth classified the rocks by how heavy they felt.

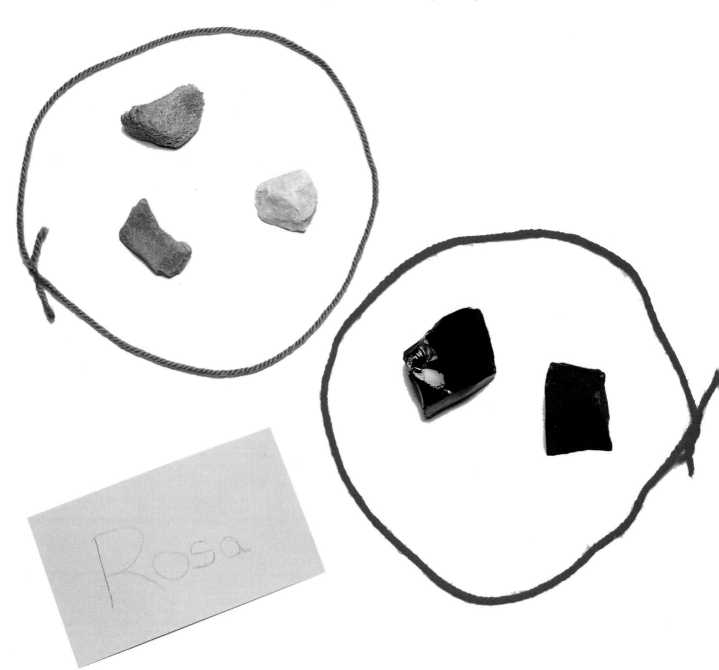

Color and "how heavy" are some **properties** of rocks. Properties are how a thing looks, feels, smells, tastes, or sounds. The properties of one kind of rock make it different from all other kinds of rocks. Rocks may be classified by their properties.

What are other properties of rocks?

Rocks have many other properties. These rocks are different shapes.

Rocks can be different sizes, too. Some are taller than buildings. Others, like grains of sand, are tiny. Why are some rocks so large and some so small? You will find out in the next lesson.

Things made with rocks can last a long time. That is because many kinds of rocks are hard. What are some things made from rocks?

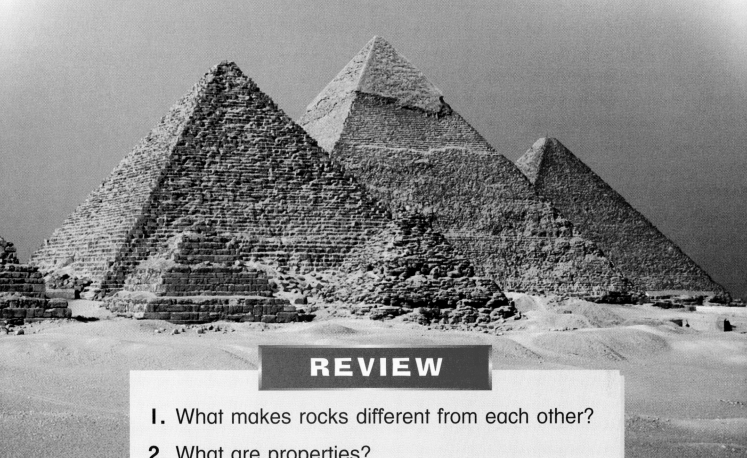

REVIEW

1. What makes rocks different from each other?

2. What are properties?

3. Name some properties of rocks.

4. **Classify** Suppose you collected a lot of rocks. You put the larger rocks in one box. You put the smaller rocks in another box. What rule did you use to classify your rocks?

5. **Think and Write** What are some famous old things made from rocks?

Why it matters

Large rocks can wear away to become small rocks.

Science Words

erosion the carrying away of rocks and soil

weathering the breaking up of rocks

Rocks Change

Did you ever find a rock along a river or a beach? Was it smooth? Did you ever look at grains of sand? How did they ever get to be so small?

Rocks come in all sizes and shapes. Something can change the size and shape of a rock.

EXPLORE

What do you think can change a rock's size and shape?

What can make a rock change?

In this activity you will try to make rocks change.

What you need

- pumice rocks
- sandpaper
- plastic jar with lid
- water
- newspaper
- *Science Journal*

What to do

1. **Observe** Rub the sandpaper on the rock. Record what happens in the *Science Journal*.

2. Put some water and rocks inside the jar. Put the lid on tightly.

3. **Predict** What will happen to the rocks if each of you shakes the jar hard? Try it.

What did you find out?

1. **Explain** What happened in steps 1 and 3?

2. **Infer** What can change rocks?

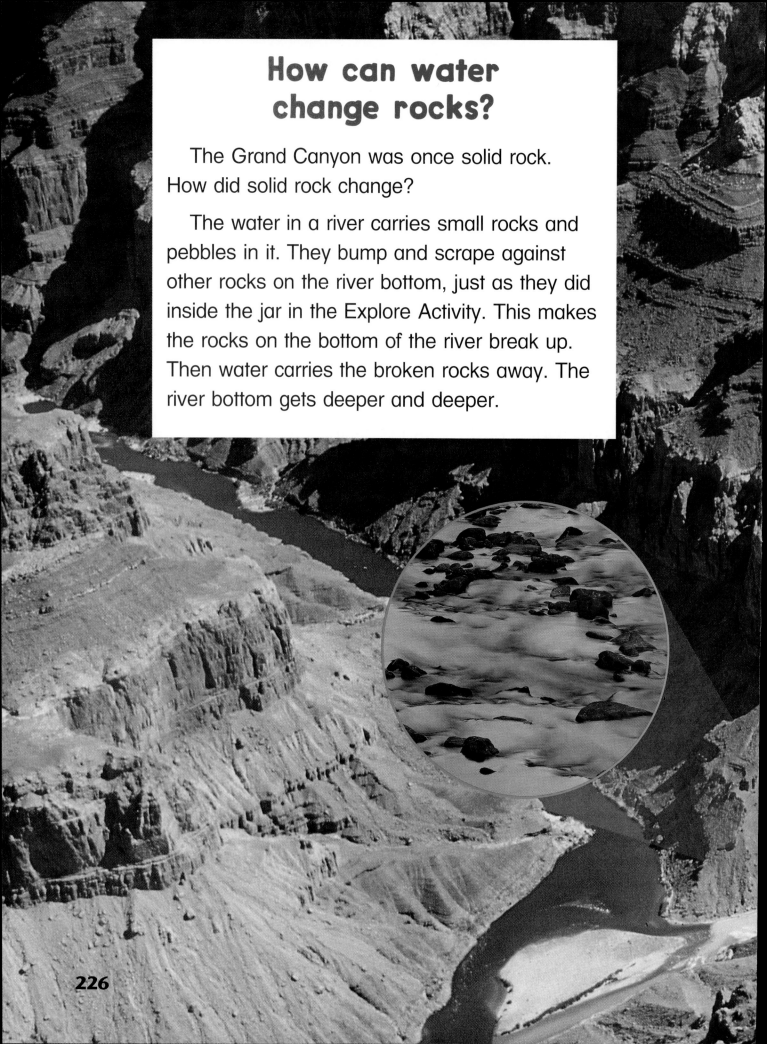

How can water change rocks?

The Grand Canyon was once solid rock. How did solid rock change?

The water in a river carries small rocks and pebbles in it. They bump and scrape against other rocks on the river bottom, just as they did inside the jar in the Explore Activity. This makes the rocks on the bottom of the river break up. Then water carries the broken rocks away. The river bottom gets deeper and deeper.

Rocks in the river break up when other rocks bump against them. The breaking up of rocks is called **weathering**.

Rocks in the river get carried away by water. The carrying away of rocks and soil is called **erosion**. Weathering and erosion work together to change rocks.

Brain Power

How long do you think it takes for weathering and erosion to change rocks?

How can wind change rocks?

You just read how water changes rocks. Wind changes rocks, too.

Like water, wind carries tiny bits of rock in it. These bits of rock hit against large rocks. This breaks up the large rocks bit by bit, a lot like the sandpaper did in the Explore Activity. Then wind blows the broken bits of rock away.

Erosion and weathering work together. They shape the land from place to place. Erosion and weathering make Earth's beautiful mountains, valleys, and canyons. They also work together to make the soil used by plants and animals.

REVIEW

1. What is erosion?

2. Name two things that cause erosion.

3. What is weathering?

4. Name two things that cause weathering.

5. **Think and Write** How do weathering and erosion work together to change rocks?

Why it matters

Some animals can get the things they need to live in a cave.

Science Words

guano droppings from bats

At Home in a Cave

Have you ever seen a cave like this one? It is not just a hole in rock. It is a home for many living things.

EXPLORE

How did the cave get here?

EXPLORE ACTIVITY

How do some caves form?

In this activity you will make a model to find out how some caves form.

What to do

1. Put the basket into the pan. Make a layer of large and small rocks.

2. Now make 3 more layers: soil, rocks, then soil.

3. **Observe** Pour 2 cups of water into the basket, then 2 more cups.

   ▨ **SAFETY** Wash your hands.

What did you find out?

1. **Observe** What happened when you poured the water? What was left?

2. **Identify** What rocky place does your model look like?

3. **Explain** How do some caves form?

What you need

- plastic basket
- rocks
- gravel
- potting mixture
- water
- pan
- newspaper
- measuring cup
- *Science Journal*

231

Why is a cave a good home for animals?

The Explore Activity shows one way a cave can form. Water washes away soil and small rocks. The cave here formed the same way.

First, water breaks up rocks. Then, water carries broken rocks away. A hole forms in the rock wall. Water makes the hole bigger. After a long time, the hole becomes a cave. A cave is a habitat where some animals can get what they need to live.

A cave protects animals from weather and from enemies. This makes a cave a good place for shelter.

A cave also has air in it which animals need. Animals need water, too, found in some caves. Water may come through cracks in the cave roof or walls. Water may also collect in pools in or near a cave.

What animals use a cave?

Many animals use caves. Bats and bears rest in caves. Snakes and other animals come here to get away from the heat or cold. These animals must leave the cave to find food.

Some animals live in a cave all the time. They find food in a cave. How? Droppings from bats are called guano (GWAH noh). Guano falls to the cave floor. Guano becomes food for the worms and beetles that live on the cave floor.

rattlesnake

black bear

bats

beetles   millipedes

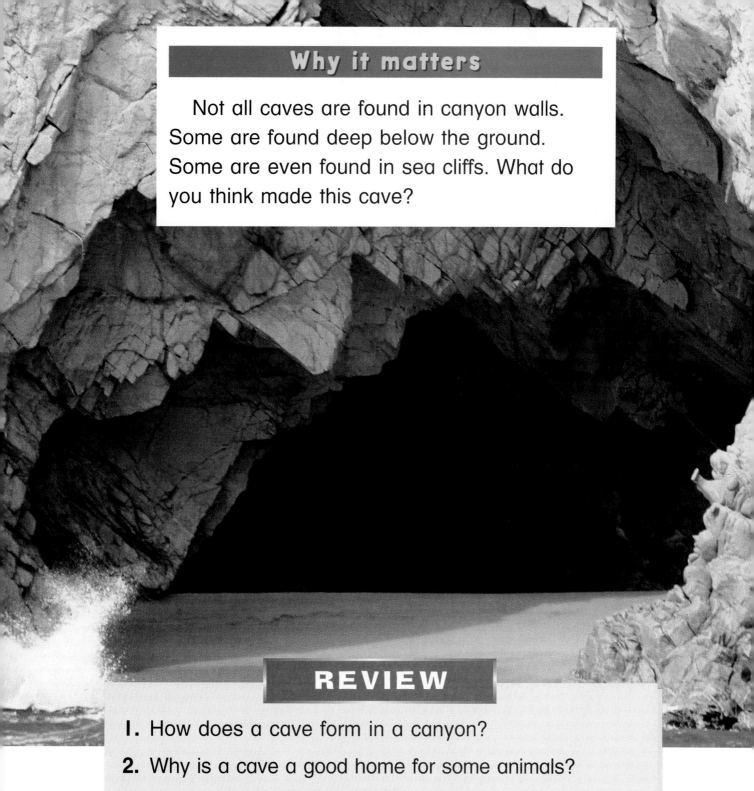

Why it matters

Not all caves are found in canyon walls. Some are found deep below the ground. Some are even found in sea cliffs. What do you think made this cave?

REVIEW

1. How does a cave form in a canyon?

2. Why is a cave a good home for some animals?

3. Name one animal that visits a cave.

4. **Infer** Why are bats important to the cave habitat?

ART LINK 5. **Think and Write** Draw a cave where an animal might live. What will you show in the cave?

235

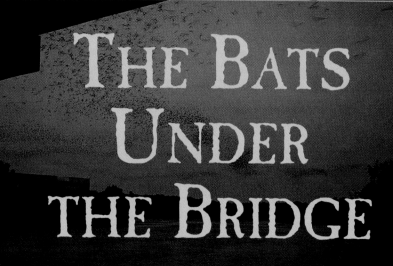

THE BATS
UNDER
THE BRIDGE

A Closer Look

Once, only a few bats lived under this bridge in Austin, Texas. Then the city repaired the bridge. There were lots of dark spaces under it. Soon it was home to thousands of bats!

Some people wanted to get rid of the bats. They thought all bats were pests. Other people wanted the bats to stay.

The city let the bats stay. Now more than a million bats live under the bridge each summer!

At night the bats leave the bridge together. They hunt for insects that destroy crops. Every night the bats eat about 13,500 kilograms (30,000 pounds) of insects. That's about the weight of four hippos!

In November, the bats fly to Mexico. They stay there all winter. In March they fly back to the bridge in Austin. It must feel good to be home!

DISCUSS

1. Why did some people want to get rid of the bats?

2. Do you think the city was right to let bats live under the bridge? Why or why not?

Use Science Words

properties
erosion
weathering
guano

1. The breaking up of rocks is called ___?___.
page 227

2. How a thing looks, feels, and smells are some of its ___?___. page 221

3. The carrying away of rocks and soil is called ___?___. page 227

4. Bat droppings are called ___?___. page 234

Use Science Ideas

5. Name some properties of rocks? pages 220-222

6. What two things break up rocks? pages 226-228

7. What two things carry rocks away? pages 226-228

8. What do living things get from caves? page 233

9. Name an animal that uses a cave. page 234

10. **Classify** You want to sort a bag of rocks. How could you group them? pages 220-221

PROBLEMS and PUZZLES

Beach Time Spread sand on a piece of paper. Observe the grains. How do you think they were formed? Could you make your own sand? How?

UNIT 5 REVIEW

Use Science Words

canyon	erosion	habitat	predator	prey	weathering

1. The place where an animal lives is its _____?_____.

2. A hawk is classified as a _____?_____ because it hunts other animals for food.

3. An animal with eyes on the sides of its head is probably a _____?_____.

4. A deep place with steep hills on either side is a _____?_____.

5. The Grand Canyon was formed by _____?_____ and by _____?_____

Use Ideas and Skills

6. Name a predator and its prey.

7. Can a puma grow up to be a sheep? Explain.

8. Tell how rocks might become smooth and round.

9.  **Classify** How would you classify these animals: a mouse, an owl, a duck, a lion?

10. Why can some kinds of beetles live in caves?

Write in Your Journal

Write about this place.

PROBLEMS and PUZZLES

Make an Animal

Design your own animal. Put together body parts like the ones shown. You may also design your own body parts. What does your animal eat? What is its habitat? Is your animal a predator or prey?

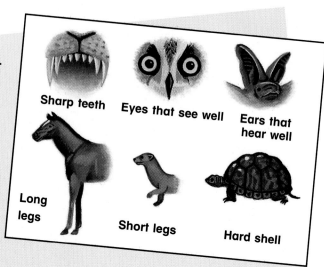

Sharp teeth   Eyes that see well   Ears that hear well

Long legs   Short legs   Hard shell

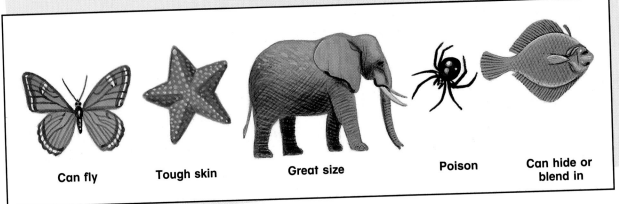

Can fly   Tough skin   Great size   Poison   Can hide or blend in

Canyon Layers

You can see layers in canyon walls. You can make a model of these layers. Pour colored sand, clay, gravel, and dirt in a glass jar. Which canyon layers are the oldest?

CHAPTER 11
YOUR HEART AND LUNGS

Why it matters

Your heart is always at work—pumping blood through your body.

Science Words

heart a muscle that is at work all the time

blood vessels tubes that carry blood

pulse the stretching of some blood vessels

blood carries nutrients, oxygen, and other things in it

Your Heart at Work

Did you ever climb a lot of stairs? Did you ever jump rope a lot? Did you ever run really fast? How did you feel when you stopped? Were you tired?

EXPLORE

Was something thumping in your chest? What do you think it was?

Can you hear a heart at work?

Does the heart beat the same way all the time? Find out.

What you need

- paper tube
- *Science Journal*

What to do

1. Place the tube on your partner's chest.

2. **Observe** Record what you hear in the *Science Journal*.

3. Have your partner jump up and down 10 times.

4. **Observe** Listen with the tube again. Record what you hear. Let your partner repeat the activity with the tube.

What did you find out?

1. **Communicate** What did you hear before your partner jumped?

2. **Contrast** How was the sound different after your partner jumped?

243

How does your heart work?

The Explore Activity shows that a person's **heart** can beat slow or fast. The heart is a muscle that is at work all the time. No other muscle in your body works harder. Your heart beats even while you sleep.

Your heart is about the size of your fist. It has spaces inside for blood.

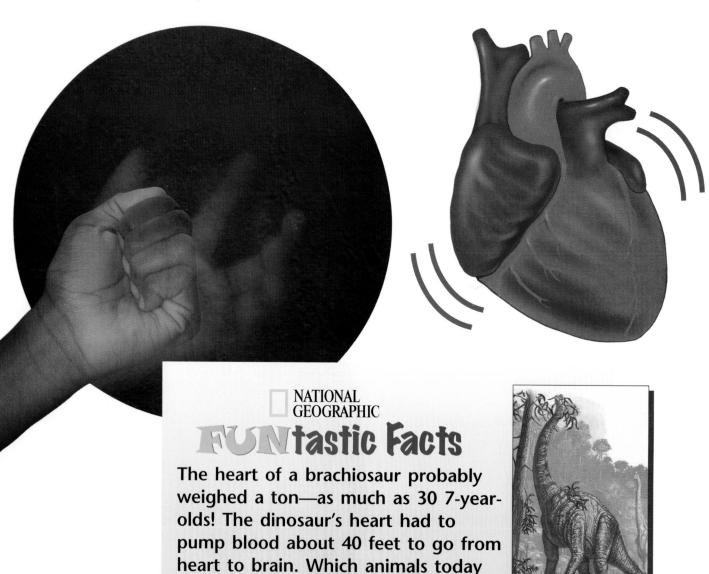

NATIONAL GEOGRAPHIC

FUNtastic Facts

The heart of a brachiosaur probably weighed a ton—as much as 30 7-year-olds! The dinosaur's heart had to pump blood about 40 feet to go from heart to brain. Which animals today do you think have large hearts?

Every time your heart beats, it pushes out the blood inside it into blood vessels. Blood vessels are tubes that carry blood from your heart to every part of your body and back to your heart again.

Some blood vessels stretch every time your heart beats. This stretching of some vessels is called your pulse. Your pulse tells you every time your heart beats. Feel your pulse in your wrist.

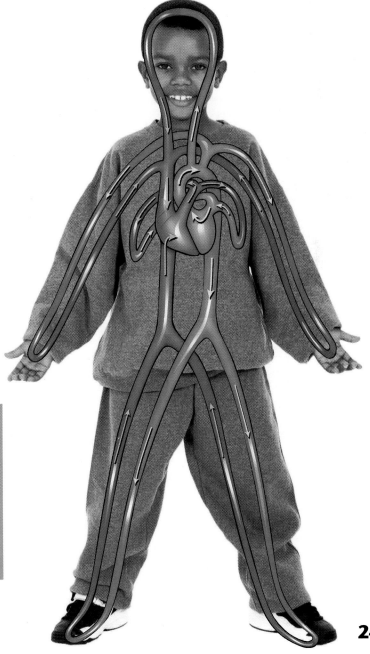

taking your pulse

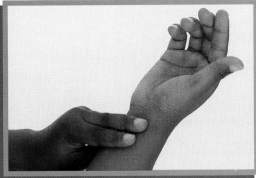

245

What can a chart tell us?

You are not the only animal with a pulse. This chart shows how fast the heart beats each minute for some animals.

Words, drawings, and photographs communicate ideas to people. Charts and graphs do, too. Charts and graphs show ideas in a way that is easy to understand.

Which animal in the chart has the most heartbeats each minute? Which has the fewest? What else does this chart tell you?

Heartbeats Each Minute

Animal	Number of heartbeats
Cat	120
Horse	44
Elephant	35
Mouse	534
Sheep	75

Communicate

In this activity you will find and chart your pulse for one minute.

What you need

- calculator (optional)

- *Science Journal*

What to do

1. **Use Numbers** Count your pulse for 30 seconds. Your teacher will show you how and will tell you when to stop counting. Record in the *Science Journal*.

2. **Use Numbers** Double this number. You may use a calculator. This is the number of heartbeats for one minute.

3. **Communicate** Show the numbers in a chart for your group.

What did you find out?

1. **Compare** Was everyone's pulse the same?

2. **Predict** What would the number of heartbeats be for other groups?

Why is blood important?

Blood fills the blood vessels. Blood carries nutrients, oxygen, and other things in it. Nutrients are the parts of food that your body uses to get energy and to grow. Oxygen (OK suh juhn) is one of many gases in the air.

As your blood flows, it carries nutrients and oxygen to every part of your body. Without nutrients and oxygen, your body cannot work. The harder your body works, the more oxygen and nutrients it needs.

Look at the picture. What parts of blood does it show?

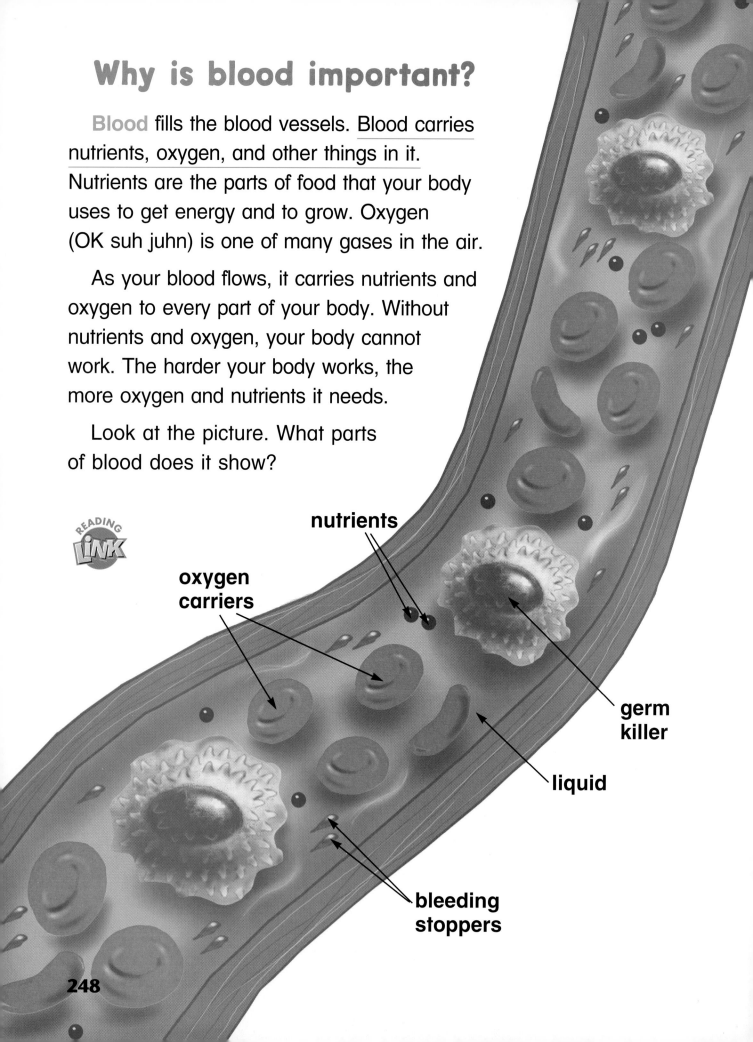

READING
LiNK

nutrients

oxygen carriers

germ killer

liquid

bleeding stoppers

One way to care for your heart is to have checkups. A doctor or nurse checks your heartbeat to find out if your heart is working just right.

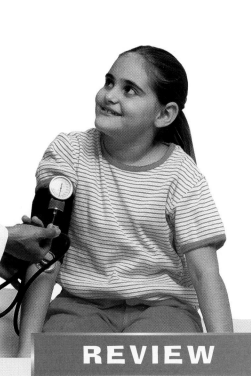

REVIEW

1. What does your heart do?

2. What is a blood vessel?

3. What does your pulse tell you?

4. **Communicate** What information does the drawing above show?

5. **Think and Write** What can you do to take care of your heart?

249

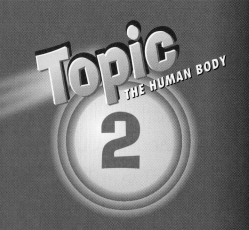
Why it matters

Your lungs are at work every time you breathe in and out.

Science Words

lungs the part of your body that takes oxygen from the air

diaphragm the main muscle used in breathing

carbon dioxide a waste gas made in your body

Your Lungs at Work

Did you ever play hard for a long time? Did you breathe in and out very fast?

Why do you breathe in and out?

EXPLORE ACTIVITY

What happens when you breathe?

Does the size of your chest change as you breathe? Find out.

What you need
- tape measure
- *Science Journal*

What to do

1. **Measure** Have a partner breathe out all the way. Measure around the chest while your partner does not breathe.

2. **Measure** Repeat. This time your partner breathes in all the way.

3. **Predict** Would the same thing happen if your partner measured you? Try it.

What did you find out?

Use Numbers Which measurement was greater? Why?

251

What happens when you breathe in?

The air all around you is made up of gases that you can't see. Oxygen is just one of them. Without oxygen, you would die quickly. To get oxygen, you breathe air into your nose or mouth. It winds up in your lungs. Lungs are the part of your body that take oxygen from the air when you breathe.

How does oxygen get to your lungs? Follow the arrows and see.

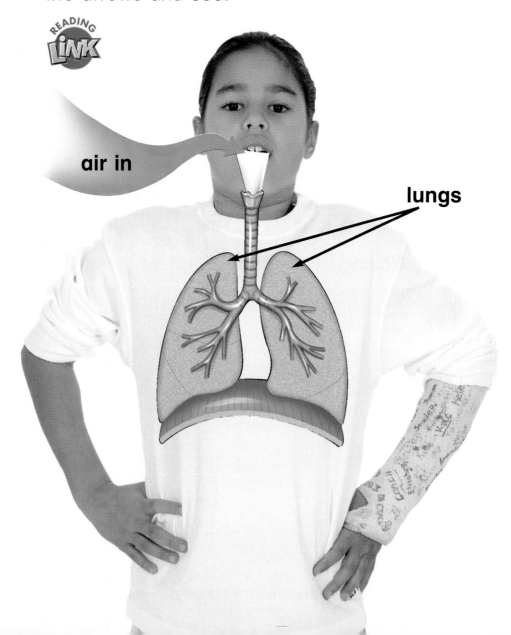

READING LINK

air in

lungs

Your lungs can't pull in air on their own. They need muscle power. The diaphragm (DYE uh fram) is the main muscle used in breathing. It is under your lungs. Muscles between the ribs in your chest also help you breathe. When you breathe in, your breathing muscles become tight. This picture shows what happens when they do.

In the Explore Activity, did you feel your chest get larger?

1 The ribs move up and out.

2 The chest and lungs get larger.

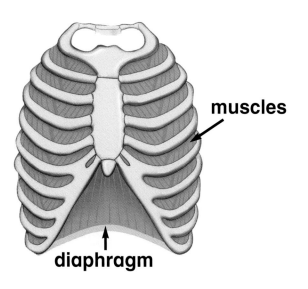

muscles

diaphragm

3 The diaphragm moves down and flattens. Air rushes into the lungs.

What happens when you breathe out?

When you breathe in, your lungs take oxygen from the air. When you breathe out, your lungs get rid of **carbon dioxide** (KAR buhn dye OK side). Carbon dioxide is a waste gas made in your body.

How does your body do this? First your breathing muscles relax. The picture shows what happens when they do.

In the Explore Activity, did you feel your chest get smaller?

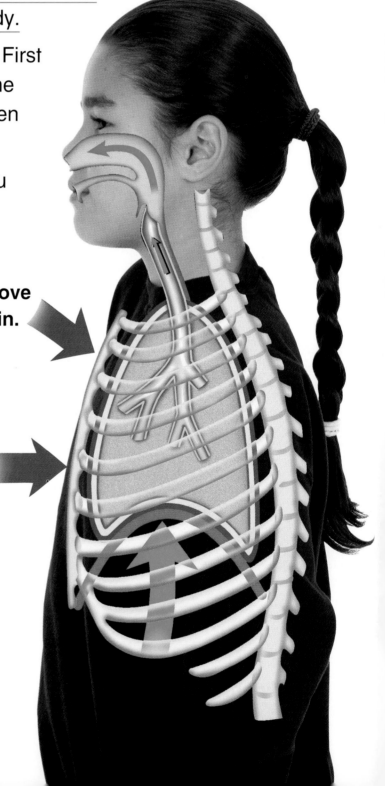

1 The ribs move down and in.

2 The chest and lungs get smaller.

3 The diaphragm moves up. Air is squeezed out of the lungs.

Your lungs are a very important part of you. They bring oxygen into your body. They get rid of carbon dioxide. Too much carbon dioxide in your body can make you sick.

REVIEW

1. Which gas does your body need to stay alive?

2. How does your body take in this gas?

3. What is the diaphragm?

4. **Communicate** Draw a picture that shows how air reaches your lungs.

5. **Think and Write** Can you forget to breathe? Explain.

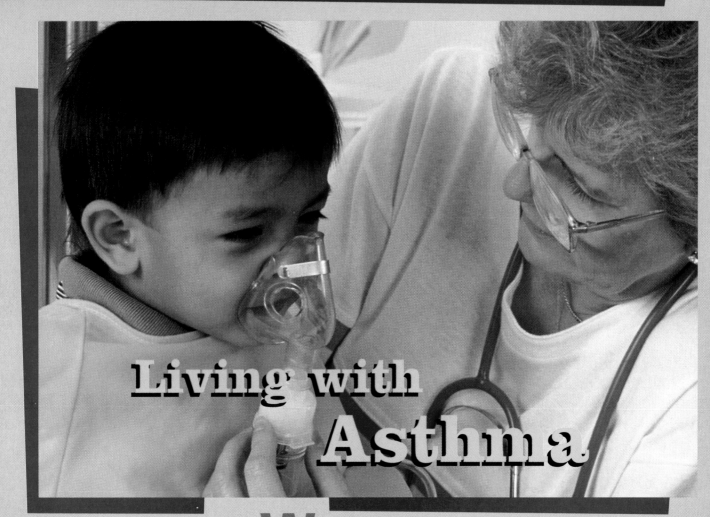

Living with Asthma

What if you suddenly had trouble breathing? That's what happens to a person with asthma.

This boy has asthma. When an asthma attack begins, he feels tightness in his chest. He coughs a lot, too.

A Closer Look

Asthma attacks occur when the tubes that carry air to the lungs swell. The swelling makes it hard for the person to breathe. Special medicine helps open the tubes.

Many people with asthma are allergic to dust and other things. These things may cause an asthma attack.

Asthma doesn't go away. With medicine, people with asthma can stay active.

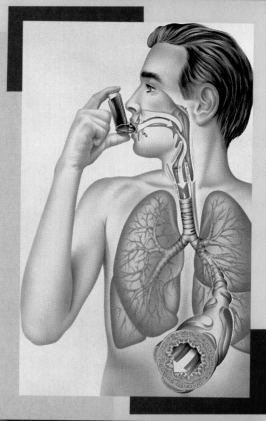

Tom Dolan won a gold medal in the Olympics. He has asthma.

Discuss

1 Why is it hard to breathe during an asthma attack?

2 Can someone with asthma play sports?

CHAPTER 11 REVIEW

Use Science Words

lungs

pulse

heart

diaphragm

carbon dioxide

blood

1. The fist-sized muscle is the ___?___. page 244

2. In your wrist you feel a ___?___. page 245

3. Your vessels are filled with ___?___. page 248

4. You breathe with ___?___. page 252

5. The main breathing muscle is the ___?___. page 253

6. You breathe out ___?___. page 254

Use Science Ideas

7. Why is your heart important? pages 244–245

8. Why is your blood important? page 248

9. Why are your lungs important? pages 252–254

10. **Communicate** What does this graph tell you?

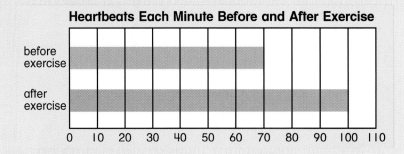

Heartbeats Each Minute Before and After Exercise

before exercise

after exercise

0   10   20   30   40   50   60   70   80   90   100   110

PROBLEMS and PUZZLES

Beat It Can feelings change your pulse rate? Next time you are scared or excited, take your pulse. Compare it to your pulse at rest.

CHAPTER 12
WORKING TOGETHER

Why it matters

The heart and lungs work together as a team.

Team Work

The race is over. You won. You ran so fast that you could not catch your breath. You feel your heart pounding.

EXPLORE

Why are your heart and lungs working so hard at the same time?

EXPLORE  ACTIVITY

Move, Move, Move

Find out how blood moves in your body.

What to do

1. Let 2 children be "blood movers." Let one child be a "muscle." Let one child be the "lungs."

2. The children who carry colored squares will be the "blood."

3. Play the game in an open space. Your teacher will tell you how.

What you need

- 50 red paper squares

- 50 blue paper squares

- 2 sheets of paper

- red paper

- blue paper

- tape

- *Science Journal*

What did you find out?

1. **Infer** Which part of your body does the job of the 2 blood movers? Record in the *Science Journal*.

2. **Explain** How does blood move in your body?

261

One pump or two?

The Explore Activity shows how a blood mover works. The heart is a blood mover. The heart pumps blood, but it is not just one pump. The heart is really two pumps. Find the dark red color in the picture. This is blood that comes from all parts of the body. It's on its way to the lungs.

Why does blood go to the lungs? Blood needs to pick up fresh oxygen from the lungs. Blood also needs to get rid of carbon dioxide.

Now find the bright red color in the picture. This is blood full of oxygen that comes from the lungs. It's going back to the heart to be pumped to every part of the body. Every time your heart beats, both sides pump. Some blood picks up fresh oxygen and some delivers it. The Explore Activity shows this.

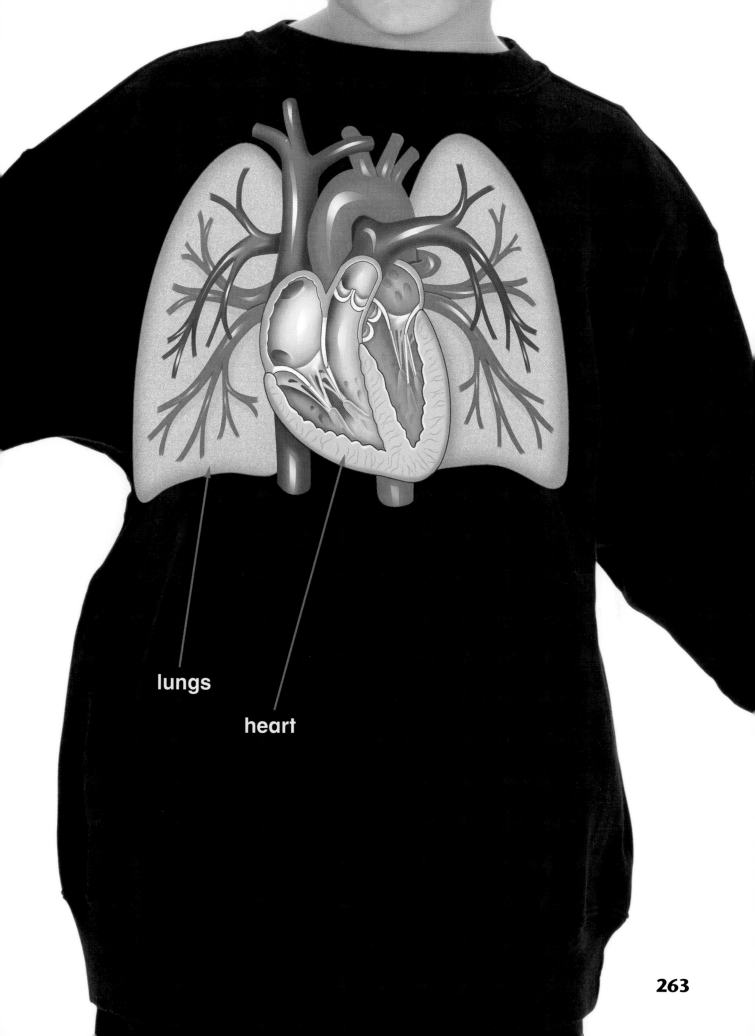

lungs

heart

How do heart and lungs work together?

What happens during a race? Your leg muscles work hard. The faster you run, the harder your muscles have to work. The harder your muscles work, the more oxygen they need, and the more carbon dioxide they must get rid of. Your lungs breathe harder to get rid of carbon dioxide and get more oxygen. Your heart pumps blood faster to your lungs and to your muscles.

Brain Power

What happens to your heart and lungs a while after the race is over?

264

You can see how your heart and lungs work together as a team. No matter what you do, they must always work together to keep you alive. Can you follow the path of blood from the heart to the lungs and to the leg muscles in this picture?

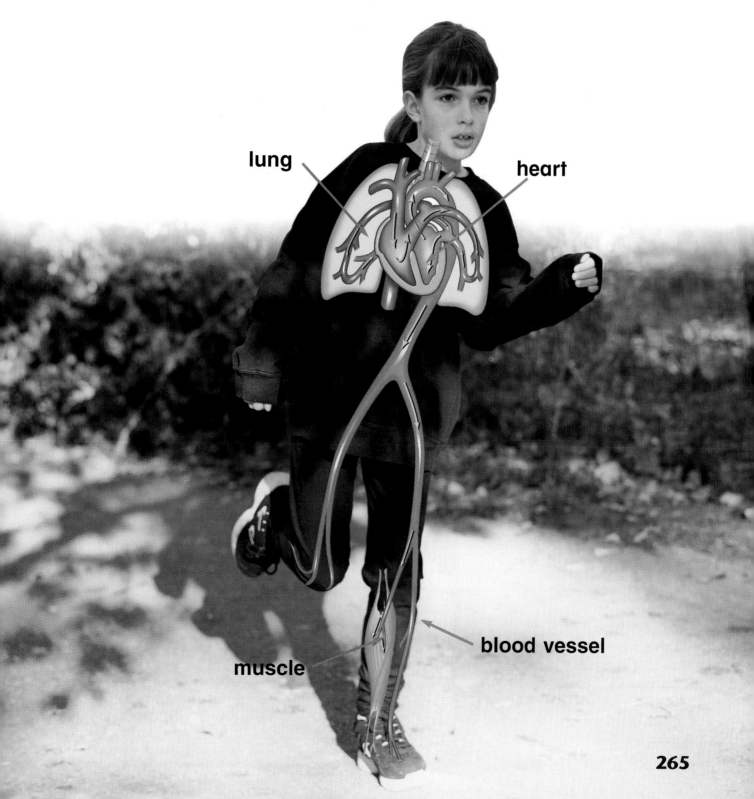

lung

heart

blood vessel

muscle

How can the heart and lungs stay fit?

You can help your heart and lungs to stay fit. How? Being active is one way. An exercise such as sit-ups is one way to be active. Being active makes the heart and lungs strong.

You also need to get rest and sleep. Your heart and lungs need to slow down each day so they won't tire out. You can also try to eat lots of fruits and vegetables.

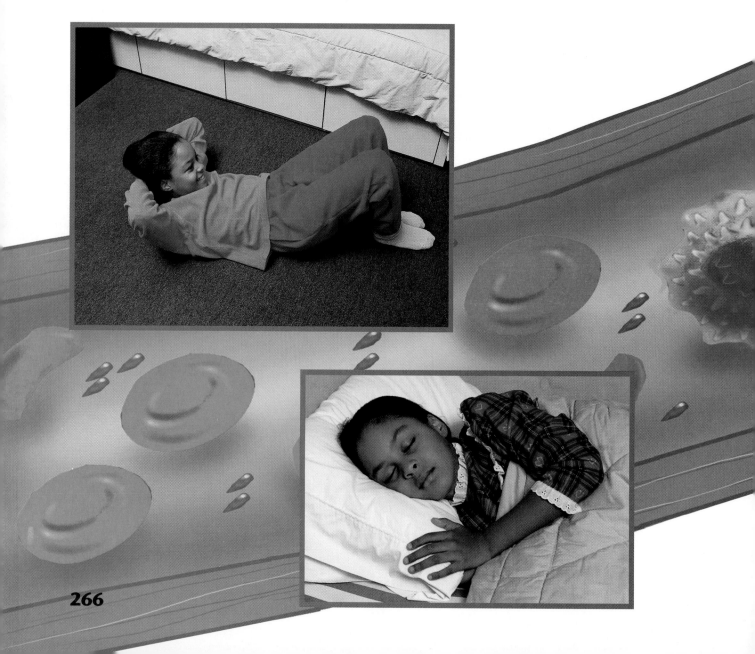

You cannot live without your heart or lungs. You need to take care of them.

REVIEW

1. What does blood do in the lungs?

2. How do the heart and lungs work together?

3. Name things you can do to take care of your heart and lungs.

4. **Infer** What things might harm your heart and lungs?

5. **Think and Write** Draw a picture of your heart and lungs. Label them.

267

Staying Safe on a Bike

How can you keep your heart and lungs strong? You can stay active. Riding a bike is one way to stay active. These rules will keep you safe while you ride.

1. Ride a bike that fits you.

2. Check your bike's safety equipment.

3. Wear a safety helmet.

4. Keep your shoes tied so the laces don't get caught in the chain.

5. Ride on the right side of the road. Stay close to the curb.

6. Always obey traffic signs and lights.

7. Before crossing a street, look left, look right, then look left again. Walk your bike across busy streets.

8. Use hand signals when turning or stopping.

9. To stop, squeeze your front and back brakes an equal amount. This way, you won't get thrown off.

10. Allow more time to stop on gravel or in the rain.

Health Link

DISCUSS

1. How can riding a bike help keep you healthy?

2. Why should you use hand signals before making a turn?

Use Science Words

Draw a line to the words that best complete each sentence.

1. The faster you run   a. oxygen to work.

2. Muscles need   b. can keep your heart fit.

3. When you breathe out   c. work together as a team.

4. Eating fruits and vegetables   d. you get rid of carbon dioxide.

5. The heart and lungs   e. the harder your muscles work.

Use Science Ideas

For questions 6–9, write *true* or *false*.

6. The heart and lungs are always working.

7. Rest is not important for the heart and lungs.

8. Being active makes the heart and lungs strong.

9. Blood gets rid of oxygen in the lungs.

10. **Infer** What gas is inside this firefighter's tank?

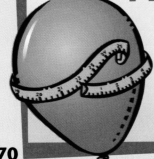

PROBLEMS and PUZZLES

Fill It Up Take a deep breath and blow up a balloon. Measure the balloon. Repeat. This time, do not take a deep breath first. What do you notice?

Use Science Words

| blood vessels | carbon dioxide | heart | lungs | pulse |

1. The muscle that pushes blood is the ___?___.

2. In your wrist, you can feel a ___?___.

3. Blood moves through tubes called ___?___.

4. Oxygen is taken from the air in your ___?___.

5. The waste gas you breathe out is ___?___.

Use Ideas and Skills

6. Why is oxygen important to you?

7. When do your lungs get larger?

8. What does your diaphragm do?

9. What does blood pick up from the lungs?

10. 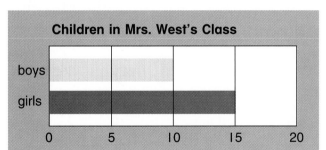 **Communicate** What does this graph tell you?

Children in Mrs. West's Class

boys

girls

0   5   10   15   20

 **Write in Your Journal**

Draw a picture of your
heart and lungs.

271

PROBLEMS AND PUZZLES

Bottle of Air

What makes you breathe? Try pushing a plastic bottle to find out. What happens to the air in the bottle when you push in? When you push out? Your lungs work like the bottle. How do you think the diaphragm works?

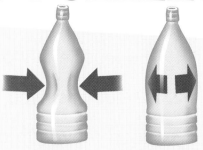

push in   push out

lungs

muscle

Health Track

How can you make sure that your heart and lungs are healthy? Keep track of three key things: (1) the amount of fruit and vegetables you eat, (2) the amount of sleep you get, and (3) how active you are. Show these in a table.

Day	Fruit and Vegetables	Sleep	Being Active
Monday	apple, banana salad	9 hours	soccer –1 hr bike 30 min
Tuesday			
Wednesday			
Thursday			

REFERENCE SECTION

PICTURE BUILDERS

Building Life Cycles

All living things go through a life cycle. A life cycle is the way a living thing grows and changes. Do all living things have the same life cycle?

BASE

Look on the next page. You will see two life cycles. How are they different? Lift up all the clear sheets (1, 2, 3). These are the overlays. The page on the bottom is the base. **What do you see on the base?**

OVERLAY 1

Drop overlay 1 down onto the base. **What happened to each life cycle?**

OVERLAY 2

Drop overlay 2 down. **Which life cycle is all done? Which still has more to go?**

OVERLAY 3

Drop overlay 3 down. **Which life cycle changed? How?**

SUM UP

How are the two life cycles alike? How are they different?

just born

 egg

BASE: Start with a baby and an egg.

PICTURE BUILDERS
Activities

1 Act Out a Picture

How could you act out the life cycle of the butterfly? How would you show each part? Use your hands. Use your legs. Use things such as towels or sheets if you need to.

2 Write an Explanation

You learned about two life cycles. Which one is like the life cycle of people? Explain your answer. Write out your ideas.

REFERENCE SECTION

Stay Safe

We need to stay safe.

Here are some safety tips.

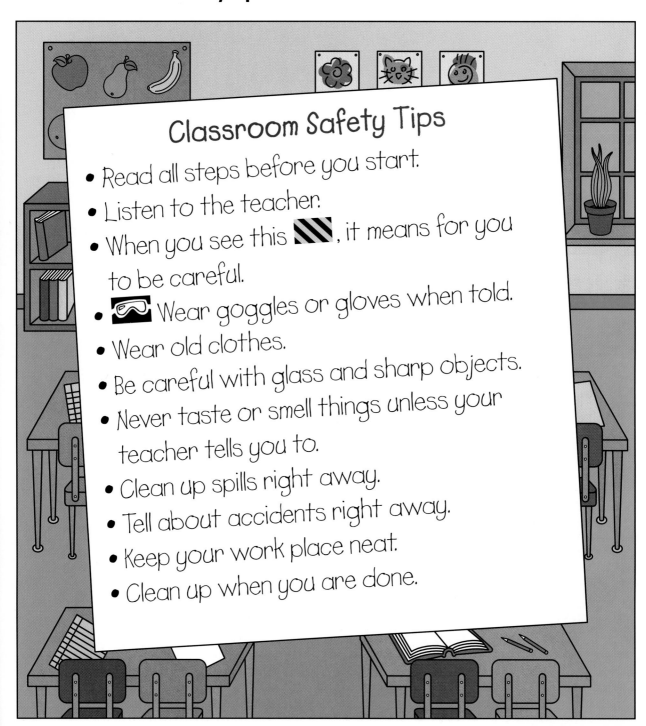

Classroom Safety Tips

- Read all steps before you start.
- Listen to the teacher.
- When you see this ▨, it means for you to be careful.
- ◨ Wear goggles or gloves when told.
- Wear old clothes.
- Be careful with glass and sharp objects.
- Never taste or smell things unless your teacher tells you to.
- Clean up spills right away.
- Tell about accidents right away.
- Keep your work place neat.
- Clean up when you are done.

Outside Safety Tips

- Listen to the teacher.
- Stay with your group.
- Never taste or smell things unless your teacher tells you to.
- Don't touch plants or animals unless your teacher tells you to.
- Put living things back where you found them.
- Tell about accidents right away.

Save and Recycle

We should not waste things.

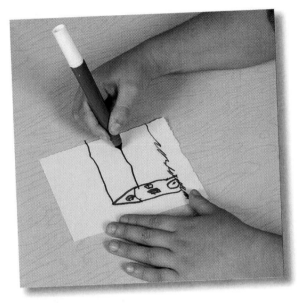

Use no more than
you need.

Don't leave the water on.

Use things more than
one time.

Recycle as much as
you can.

Clean Up

We need to clean up work places.

Let an adult clean up broken glass.

Pour water into a sink, not into a trash can.

Don't get paint or food on you.

Put food in plastic bags. This keeps bugs away.

Care of Plants

Here are ways to care for plants.

- Give plants water and sunlight.
- Ask the teacher before you touch or eat a plant. Some plants will make you very sick.
- Don't dig up plants or pick flowers. Let plants grow where they are.

Care of Animals

Here are ways to care for animals.

- Give animals food and water. Give them a safe place to live, too.
- Be kind to animals. Handle them with care.
- Look at wild animals. Don't touch them. They may bite, sting, or scratch.
- Leave the places where animals live alone.

How to Measure

You can use many things to measure.

This string is about 8 paper clips long.

This string is about 3 pencils long.

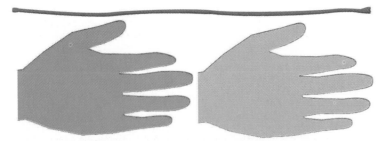

This string is about 2 hands long.

Try It

1. Measure some string. Tell how you did it.
2. Can you measure string with these paper clips? Why or why not?

Units of Measurement

People don't measure with paper clips.

They use centimeters (cm) or meters (m).

These are called units of measurement.

The crayon is about 8 centimeters long.

We write this as 8 cm.

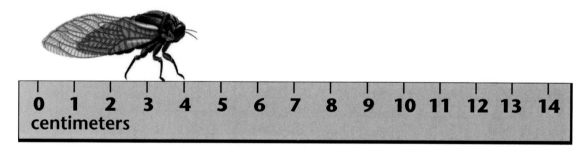

The bug is about 4 centimeters long.

We write this as 4 cm.

Try It

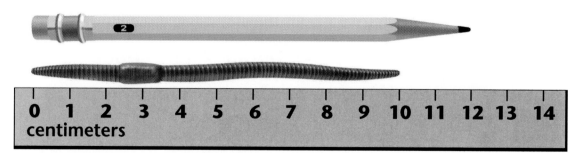

1. How long is the pencil?

2. How long is the worm?

Use a Ruler

| 0 1 2 3 4 5 6 7 8 9 10 11 12 13 14 |
| centimeters |

You can use a ruler to measure this leaf.
Line up the end of the leaf with the 0 on
the ruler.
The leaf is about 11 centimeters or 11 cm.

Try It

Find each object.
Estimate how long.
Use a ruler to measure.

	Estimate	Measure
? (pencil)	about ? cm	about ? cm
? (book)	about ? cm	about ? cm
? (calculator)	about ? cm	about ? cm

Use a Meterstick

A meterstick is 1 meter or
100 centimeters long.
This dog is about 1 meter tall.

A meterstick is used to measure
long or tall objects.
Use a meterstick just like a ruler.

Try It

Estimate how high or long.
Use a meterstick to measure.

	Estimate	Measure
?	about ? m	about ? m
?	about ? m	about ? m
?	about ? m	about ? m

Use a Thermometer

A thermometer measures temperature.

It gets warmer. The liquid in a thermometer moves up.

It gets cooler. The liquid in a thermometer moves down.

Which thermometer shows a warmer temperature? How can you tell?

A 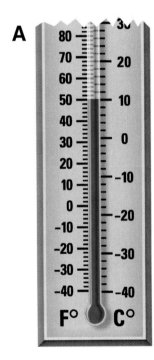   B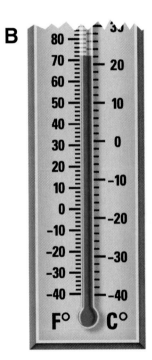

A thermometer has marks with numbers.
This thermometer shows degrees Fahrenheit and degrees Celsius.
Each mark means 2 degrees.

Read this thermometer in degrees Celsius.
Find the number just below where the liquid ends.
The number is 20.
Count on 2 degrees for each mark after 20 as: 22, 24, 26.
The thermometer shows 26 degrees Celsius, or 26° C.

Try It
What temperatures are shown on page R12?

Use a Measuring Cup

Volume is the amount of space something takes up.
Use a measuring cup to find volume.
There are 200 milliliters (200 mL) of water in this cup.

Try It

1. Get 3 different small containers.

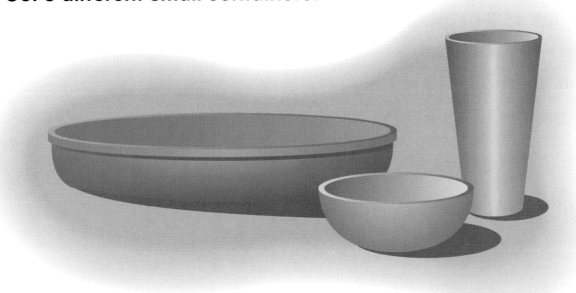

2. Which holds the most? Which holds the least?

3. Fill each container with water. Pour the water into the measuring cup. Find the volumes.

Use a Balance

A balance compares mass.

Before you compare mass, make sure the arrow points to the line.

Place an object on each pan.
The object that has more mass will make that side of the balance go down.
The object that has less mass will make that side of the balance go up.

Try It

1. Place 2 objects on a balance.
2. Which has more mass?

Try It

1. Place 3 objects in order from least mass to most mass.
2. Use the balance to check.

Use a Clock

A clock measures time.
Each mark means I minute.
There are 5 minutes between each number.
There are 60 minutes in I hour.

hour hand   minute hand

30 minutes after 1 o'clock
1:30

5 minutes after 9 o'clock
9:05

Try It

How long do you think it takes to write your name 5 times? Have a friend time you.

R16

Use a Hand Lens

A hand lens makes objects seem larger.

To use a hand lens:

Step 1: Move the lens away from the object.
Stop when the object looks fuzzy.

Step 2: Move the lens a little closer
to the object.
Stop when the object looks clear.

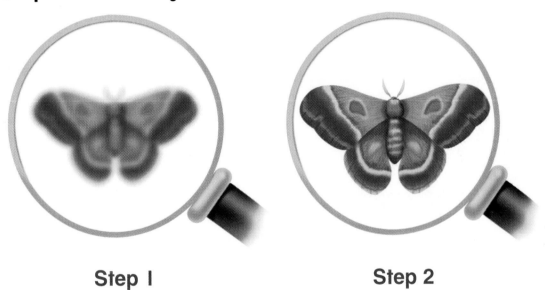

Step 1   Step 2

Try It

1. Observe each animal.
   Use a hand lens.

spider

fly

2. How many legs do you see on the spider?

3. What else can you see?

Use a Computer

A computer is a tool that can get information.

You can use the Internet. The Internet links your computer to ones far away.

You can also use CD-ROMs. They have a lot of information. You can fit many books on one CD-ROM!

Try It

1. Use the Internet. Find out how warm it is where you live.
2. Use the Internet. Find out how warm it is in a different place.

Record and Compare

You can write information in a chart.
You can use this information.

This chart shows information about
leaves that some children found.

Name	smooth-edged leaves 	saw-toothed leaves 
Mark	4	6
Kim	5	5
Bonnie	3	7

Try It

1. How many children found leaves?
2. What kinds of leaves did the children find?
3. How many leaves did Bonnie find?

Observe Parts

The parts of a machine work together.

Try It

Name the parts of each machine.

How Parts Work Together

A machine needs all its parts to work.

What part is missing?

GLOSSARY

A

attract pull *(page 178)*

A magnet can attract **some kinds of metal.**

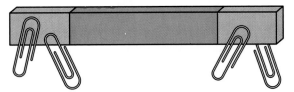

B

blood carries nutrients, oxygen, and other things in it *(page 248)*

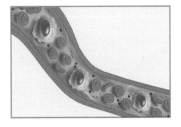

blood vessels tubes that carry blood *(page 245)*

C

canyon a deep place with steep hills on either side *(page 196)*

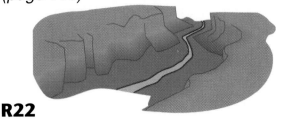

carbon dioxide (KAR buhn dye OK side), a waste gas made in your body *(page 254)*

Cenozoic Era (see nuh ZOH ik) the "Age of Mammals" *(page 84)*

classify to group things that are alike in some way *(page 198)*

You can classify **buttons by color.**

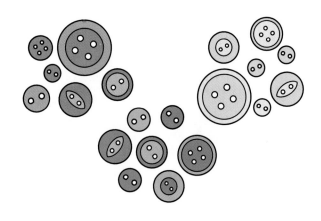

R22

condenses changes from a gas back to a liquid *(page 29)*

Water condenses on the glass.

conserve save *(page 41)*

The boy can conserve water by turning it off.

constellation a pattern of stars *(page 124)*

D

diaphragm (DYE uh fram) the main muscle used in breathing *(page 253)*

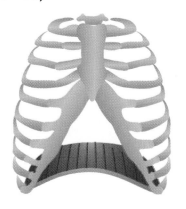

E

endangered living things close to becoming extinct *(page 90)*

The manatee is endangered.

era a very long amount of time *(page 82)*

erosion the carrying away of rocks and soil *(page 227)*

evaporates changes to a gas in air *(page 28)*

Water in this puddle evaporates.

extinct to die out *(page 83)*

Dinosaurs are extinct.

F

food chain how energy from food passes from one living thing to another *(page 74)*

force a push or a pull *(page 148)*

It takes force to move the box.

fossil imprint and remains of something that lived long ago *(page 53)*

friction (FRIK shuhn) the rubbing of one thing on another *(page 158)*

Friction warms her hands.

fruit the plant part that holds the seeds *(page 12)*

fuel a thing that gives off heat when burned *(page 104)*

Wood is a kind of fuel.

fulcrum the point that holds up the bar of a lever *(page 162)*

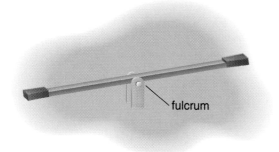

fulcrum

G

gravity a force that pulls between things and Earth *(page 149)*

Gravity **pulls her down.**

guano (GWAH noh) droppings from bats *(page 234)*

H

habitat a place where a plant or animal lives *(page 200)*

heart a muscle that is at work all the time *(page 244)*

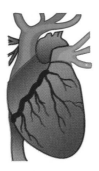

heat energy that can make things change *(page 100)*

Heat **changes the candle.**

I

imprint a mark that is made when an object presses into something *(page 52)*

infer to use what you know to figure something out *(page 54)*

L

leaves plant parts that grow from the stem *(page 5)*

lever (LEV ur) a simple machine used to change the force needed to lift things *(page 162)*

life cycle a pattern of growth that happens over and over again *(page 8)*

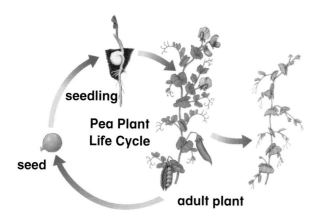

Pea Plant Life Cycle
seedling
seed
adult plant

light a kind of energy *(page 118)*

We get light from the Sun.

lungs the part of your body that takes oxygen from the air *(page 252)*

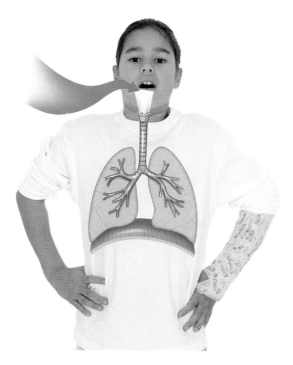

M

magnetic field (mag NET ik feeld) the place around a magnet where its force pulls or pushes *(page 186)*

measure find the size or amount of something *(page 102)*

The measure of the paper clip is about 5 centimeters.

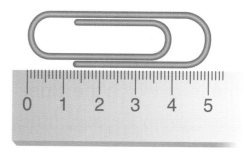

Mesozoic era (mez uh ZOH ik) the "Age of Reptiles" *(page 84)*

moon phases the different shapes of the Moon *(page 126)*

N

natural resources things that come from Earth *(page 40)*

> Water, air, and soil are natural resources.

O

observe use your senses to learn about something *(page 6)*

P

paleontologist (pale ee uhn TOL uh jist) a person who studies life in the past *(page 66)*

Paleozoic era (pay lee uh ZOH ik) time from which the oldest plant and animal fossils have been found *(page 83)*

pitch how high or how low a sound is *(page 131)*

> A drum has a low pitch.

poles the places of a magnet where its pull is strongest *(page 179)*

> A magnet has two poles.

S   N

pollute make dirty *(page 42)*

> People pollute land and water.

predator an animal that hunts another animal for food *(page 206)*

The puma is a predator.

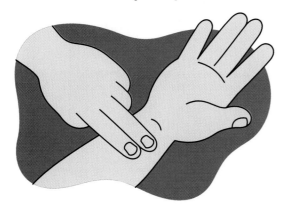

prey animals that are hunted *(page 206)*

The sheep is the prey.

properties how a thing looks, feels, smells, tastes, or sounds *(page 221)*

pulse the stretching of some blood vessels *(page 245)*

You can feel your pulse.

pupa (PYOO puh) the stage before the adult butterfly *(page 211)*

R

ramp a simple machine with a slanted surface *(page 169)*

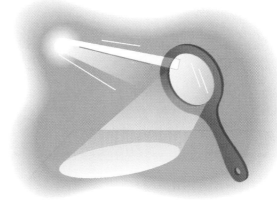

reflect bounce off *(page 120)*

A mirror can reflect light.

GLOSSARY

repel push away *(page 180)*

These magnets repel.

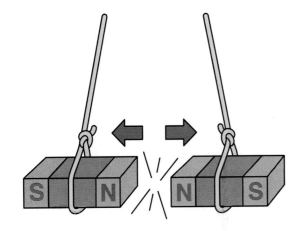

roots plant parts that grow under the ground *(page 4)*

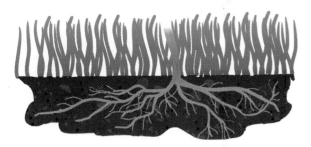

S

shelter a place where animals can be safe from their enemies *(page 69)*

simple machine anything that can change the direction and size of forces *(page 162)*

A ramp is a simple machine.

skeleton a body frame made of bones *(page 66)*

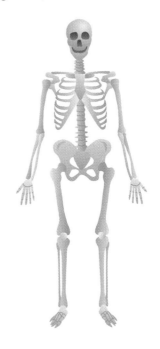

sound a kind of energy *(page 130)*

The bell makes sound.

stem holds the plant up straight
(page 5)

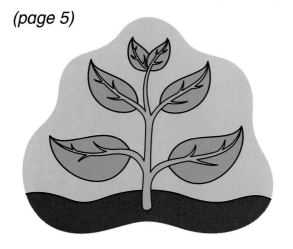

T

temperature how warm or cold something is *(page 101)*

The temperature is cold here.

thermometer a tool that measures temperature
(page 102)

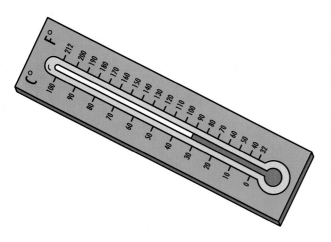

V

vibrate move back and forth quickly *(page 130)*

You can see the strings vibrate.

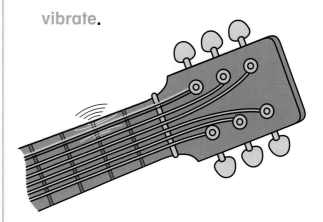

W

water cycle the moving of water between Earth and sky over and over again *(page 30)*

weathering the breaking up of rocks *(page 227)*

The rock shows weathering by the roots of plants.

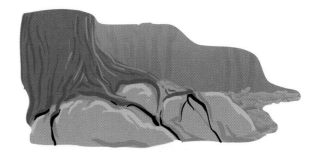

CREDITS

Design & Production: Kirchoff/Wohlberg, Inc.

Cover: Paul Howell/Liaison International.

Maps: Geosystems.

Transvision: David Mager (photography); Mike DiGiorgio, Wendy Smith (illustration).

Illustration Credits: Ka Botzis: pp. 20, 34–35, 47, 66–67, 68; Barbara Cousins: pp. 245, 252, 253, 254, 263, 265, 272; Marie Dauenheimer: pp. 244, 248, 266–267; Mike DiGiorgio: pp. 140–141. Jeff Fagan: pp. 51, 114, 121, 130, 142, 159, 174; Russell Farrell: p.88; Kristen Goeters: pp. 156–157, 261, 272; Virge Kask: pp. 5, 8, 24, 46; Katie Lee: pp. 18, 19, 30; Tom Leonard: pp. 60–61, 72–73, 74, 206, 234, 204–205, 240; Claude Martinot: pp. 9, 48, 192; Monika Popowitz: pp. 21, 37, 57, 64, 69; Pat Rasch: pp. 41, 42; Wendy Smith: pp. 211, 212, 216, 238; Craig Spearing: p. S17; Matt Straub: pp. 71, 83, 84, 88, 94, 96, 110, 246, 258, 270, 271; Ted Williams: pp. 82, 105, 124–125, 136, 179, 180, 190, 191. Handbook: Bateman: pp. R10, R11, R14, R19; Rita Lascaro: pp. R2, R3, R6, R7; Rob Schuster: pp. R12, R13, R20, R21; Ted Williams: pp.R8, R9, R16–R18. Glossary: Batelman: pp. R23, R24, R25, R26, R27, R28, R29, R30; Rita Lascaro: pp. R22, R23, R24, R25, R26, R28, R29, R30, R31; Mike DiGiorgio: pp. R22, R23, R24, R25, R26, R28, R29, R30, R31

Photography Credits:

Contents: iii: Stephen P. Parker/Photo Researchers, Inc. iv: H.G.Ross/FPG International. v: Eunice Harris/Photo Researchers, Inc. vi: David Lawrence/ The Stock Market. vii: Pat Caulfield/Photo Researchers, Inc. viii: Howard Sochurek/The Stock Market.

National Geographic Invitation to Science: S2: Chuck Nicklin/Sea Films, Inc. S3: t, Nancy Sefton/Photo Researchers, Inc.; m, Al Giddings; b, Natalie Fobes.

Be a Scientist: S5: David Mager. S6: Gianni Tortoli/Photo Researchers, Inc. S7: t, Dave Bartruff/Stock, Boston; b, Francois Gohier/Photo Researchers, Inc. S8: Ruben G. Mendoza. S9: Ruben G. Mendoza. S10: l, The Granger Collection; r, Leo Touchet. S11: David Hiser/Tony Stone Worldwide. S12: Ruben G. Mendoza. S13: t, Robert E. Daemmrich/ Tony Stone Worldwide; b, Wil Yurman/The Gamma Liaison Network. S14: Ruben G. Mendoza. S15: Gabe Palmer/The Stock Market. S16: Niklas Hill/Gamma Liaison. S18: t, Peter Correz/Tony Stone Images; b, Scott Harvey/MMSD. S19: t, Crews/The Image Works; b, Chip Henderson/ Tony Stone Worldwide. S20: t, Richard Hutchings/PhotoEdit.

Unit 1: 1: Zefa/Stock Imagery, Inc. 2: b. Marcus Brooke/FPG; t. Stan Osolinski/FPG 3: David Mager. 4: t. David Mager; b. G. Buttner/Naturbild/ Photo Researchers, Inc. 6: Hans Reinhard/Bruce Coleman, Inc. 7: David Mager. 9: l. PhotoDisc; c. David Mager; r. Jeff Greenberg/Photo Researchers, Inc. 10: Stephen Dalton/Animals Animals. 11: David Mager. 12: l. Merlin D. Tuttle/Photo Researchers, Inc.; r. Michael Fogden/Bruce Coleman, Inc. 13: Donald Specker/Animals Animals. 14: b.l. H. Taylor/OSF/ Animals Animals; r.t. Renee Lynn/Photo Researchers, Inc. 15: Gregory K. Scott/Photo Researchers, Inc. 16: David Mager. 17: David Mager. 22: Pat Lanza Field. 23: t. Cotton Coulson; r. Stephen St. John. 25: bkgrd, Gerry Ellis/ENP Images; inset, Roy Morsch/The Stock Market. 26: Jim Cummins/FPG. 27: David Mager. 28: Albano Guatti/The Stock Market. 29: David Mager. 31: Lowell Georgia/Photo Researchers, Inc. 32: David Mager. 33: David Mager. 36: t. Jerry Irwin/Photo Researchers, Inc.; b. Michael P. Gadomski/Photo Researchers, Inc. 37: David Mager. 38: Ariel Skelley/The Stock Market. 39: David Mager. 40: bkgrd, NASA; t.l. Douglas Faulkner/ Photo Researchers, Inc.; b.r. Jim Steinberg/Photo Researchers, Inc. 43: Joe Monroe/Photo Researchers, Inc.; John S. Flannery/Bruce Coleman, Inc. 44: Jerome Yeats/Science Photo Library/Photo Researchers, Inc. 44–45: Picture Perfect. 45: Rick Poley/Visuals Unlimited. 47: David Mager.

Unit 2: 49: inset, James L. Amos/Corbis; bkgrd, Tom Bean/Corbis. 50: Gordon R. Gainer/The Stock Market. 51: David Mager. 52: t. J. Beckett/ Courtesy American Museum of Natural History; b.l. James L. Amos/Photo Researchers, Inc.; b.r. Wendell Metzen/Bruce Coleman, Inc. 53: Chip Clark/Museum of Natural History, Smithsonian Institution. 53: David Mager. 54: David Mager. 55: David Mager. 58: Wayne Lynch/DRK Photo. 61: t. James L. Amos; , inset, Dave Jackson/Museum of the Rockies. 62: b. Chris Johns/Tony Stone Images; t. Johnny Johnson/Animals Animals. 63: r. Art Wolfe/Tony Stone Images; l. Francois Gohier/Photo Researchers, Inc. 65: David Mager. 70: David Mager. 71: David Mager. 75: l. Bradley Simmons/ Bruce Coleman, Inc.; r. Jen & Des Bartlett/Bruce Coleman, Inc. 76: l. Arthur Gurmankin/Phototake/PNI; c.&r. The Granger Collection, New York. 77: t. John Sibbick; b. Joe Bailey. 78: Charles R. Belinky/Photo Researchers, Inc. 79: inset, Arthur Tilley/Photo Researchers, Inc.; bkgrd, Picture Perfect. 81: David Mager. 82: Jim Steinberg/Photo Researchers, Inc. 84–85: Russ Farrell. 86: Leonard. Lee Rue III/Bruce Coleman, Inc. 87: Charles R. Belinky/Photo Researchers, Inc. 89: r. M.J. Tyler/A.N.T. Photo Library; l. P.W. Skyes, Jr./Academy of Natural Sciences/Vireo. 90: l. Douglas Faulkner/The Stock Market; r. Jeff Lepore/Photo Researchers, Inc. 91: Tim Davis/Photo Researchers, Inc. 92–93: Jane Burton/Bruce Coleman, Inc. 95: James L. Amos/Photo Researchers, Inc.

Unit 3: 97: inset, John M. Burnley/Bruce Coleman, Inc.; Tom Brakefield/ Bruce Coleman, Inc. 98: Peter Gridley/FPG. 99: David Mager. 100: Dana Buckley/The Stock Market. 100–101: Adam Jones/Dembinsky Photo. 101: Brady Monkmeyer. 102: t. & m. David Mager; b. Thomas Ives. 103: David Mager. 104: l. & r. David Mager; b. Phil Fames/Photo Researchers, Inc. 105: Jonathan Wright/Bruce Coleman, Inc. 106: David Mager. 107: David Mager. 108: David Mager. 109: David Mager. 111: David Mager. 112: t. Michael L. Smith; b. Jerome Wexler/Photo Researchers, Inc. 113: t. Mickey Pfleger 1991/PNI; b. Steve Benbow/Stock, Boston/PNI. 115: inset, Kent Miles/FPG; Rafael Marcia/Photo Researchers, Inc. 116: b.l. & b.r. David Mager; IFA/Bruce Coleman, Inc.; t.l. & t.r. Jerry Schad/Photo Researchers, Inc. 117: David Mager. 118: Frank Rossotto/The Stock Market. 119: b. David Mager; t. Skip Moody/Dembinsky Photo. 120: David Mager. 121: t.r. David Brooks/The Stock Market; t.l. David Mager. 122: Roger Ressmeyer/Corbis. 123: David Mager. 126: b. David Mager; t.c. John Sanford/Science Photo Library/Photo Researchers, Inc.; t.l. & t.r. S, Nielsen/Bruce Coleman, Inc. 127: Mount Wilson and Palomar Observatories/Photo Researchers, Inc. 128: John Shaw/Bruce Coleman, Inc. 129: David Mager. 130: David Mager. 131: t.r. Al Francekevich/The Stock Market; b.l. Jeff Greenberg/Visuals Unlimited. 132: b.l. Hans Reinhard/Bruce Coleman, Inc.; b.r. J. Barry O'Rourke/The Stock Market; t.r. Zefa Germany/The Stock Market. 133: Kaluzny/Thatcher/Tony Stone Images. 134: David Mager. 135: David Mager. 137: Arthur Morris/Visuals Unlimited; 137: t.r. Arthur Morris/Visuals Unlimited; b. David Mager. 138: Jim Cummins/FPG. 139: Martin Jones/Ecoscene/Corbis. 143: Peter French/Bruce Coleman, Inc. 144: David Mager.

Unit 4: 145: Michael Kevin Daly. 146: David Mager. 147: David Mager. 148: b.l. David Mager; t.r. Pat Farley/Monkmeyer. 149: Ed Bock/The Stock Market. 150: t.r. Brad Simmons/Bruce Coleman, Inc.; b.l. D. Brewster/Bruce Coleman, Inc. 151: David Mager. 152: David Mager. 153: David Mager. 154: David Mager. 155: David Mager. 156–157: bkgrd, Welzenbach/The Stock Market. 158: t. Norbert Schafer/The Stock Market; b. Peter Essick/Aurora/ PSI. 160: David Mager. 161: David Mager. 162: David Mager. 163: David Mager. 164: David Mager. 165: l. Joe Bator/The Stock Market; r. Rita Nannini/Photo Researchers, Inc. 166: Charles E. Rotkin/Corbis. 167: David Mager. 168: David Mager. 169: David Mager. 170: t. Matt Bradley/Bruce Coleman, Inc.; m. Ray Soto/The Stock Market; b. Richard Olivier/Corbis. 171: Debra P. Hershkowitz. 172: Bob Daemmrich/Stock, Boston/PNI. 173: t. Nettie Burke; Jane Hurd (art); b. Karen Kuehn. 175: David Mager. 176: David Mager. 177: David Mager. 178: David Mager. 181: David Mager. 182: David Mager. 183: David Mager. 184: David Mager. 185: David Mager. 186: David Mager. 187: Tom Van Sant/Photo Researchers, Inc. 188–189: FPG.

Unit 5: 193: inset, Renee Lynn/Photo Researchers, Inc.; bkgrd, Wetmore/ Photo Researchers, Inc. 194: Kunio Owaki/The Stock Market. 195: David Mager. 196: b. Edgar T. Jones/Bruce Coleman, Inc.; t. Rod Planck/Photo Researchers, Inc. 197: t. Bates Littlehales/Animals Animals; b. Jeff Lepore/ Photo Researchers, Inc. 198: David Mager. 199: David Mager. 200: b. David Noble/FPG; t.r. Geoffrey Clifford/Woodfin Camp & Associates; inset, Jeff Hoffman/Bruce Coleman, Inc. 201: John S. Flannery/Bruce Coleman, Inc. 202: Tom Brakefield/Bruce Coleman, Inc. 203: David Mager. 204: t.l. inset, Breck P. Kent/Animals Animals; b.r. inset, Brian Milne/Animals Animals. 205: t.l. inset, David H. Ellis/Visuals Unlimited; b.r. inset, Robert J. Erwin/Photo Researchers, Inc. 207: Cosmos Blank/Photo Researchers, Inc. 208: Gerard Lacz/Animals Animals. 209: David Mager. 210: t.r. inset, Jane Burton/Bruce Coleman, Inc.; b. S. Nielsen/Bruce Coleman, Inc. 212: PhotoDisc. 213: b.l. Debra P. Hershkowitz/Bruce Coleman, Inc.; t.r. Ronnie Kaufman/The Stock Market. 214: Andy Rouse. 215: t. Galen A. Rowell; b. Michael Ventura. 216: Tom Leonard. 217: bkgrd, B & C Calhoun/Bruce Coleman, Inc.; inset, John Shaw/Bruce Coleman, Inc. 218: Linda Bartlett/ Photo Researchers, Inc. 219: David Mager. 220: David Mager. 221: David Mager. 222: inset, David Mager; bkgrd, Tim Davis/Photo Researchers, Inc. 223: PhotoDisc. 224: David Mager. 225: David Mager. 226: Richard J. Green/Photo Researchers, Inc. 226–227: bkgrd, Jeff Gnass/The Stock Market. 228: John Mead/Science/Photo Researchers, Inc. 229: r. David Halpern/Photo Researchers, Inc.; l. inset, Jim Zipp/Photo Researchers, Inc. 230: George H. H. Huey/Animals Animals Earth Scenes. 231: David Mager. 232: Rod Planck/Photo Researchers, Inc. 233: C.C. Lockwood/Animals Animals. 235: Gregory G. Dimijian/Photo Researchers, Inc. 236–237: Merlin D. Tuttle/Photo Researchers, Inc. 236: inset, Guillermo Gonzale Visuals Unlimited. 237: George Bryce/Animals Animals. 239: Kenneth Murray/Photo Researchers, Inc..

Unit 6: 241: David Mager. 242: Debra P. Hershkowitz. 243: David Mager. 244: David Mager. 245: David Mager. 247: David Mager. 249: David Mager. 250: Tom & Dee Ann/The Stock Market. 251: David Mager. 252: David Mager. 253: David Mager. 254: David Mager. 255: David Mager. 256: Larry Mulvehill/Photo Researchers, Inc. 257: t. John Bavosi/SPL/Photo Researchers, Inc.; b. Todd Warshaw/AllSport. 259: bkgrd, Comstock KLIPS; inset, Elyse Lewin/The Image Bank.260: David Mager. 262–263: David Mager. 264–265: David Mager. 266: David Mager. 267: David Mager. 268–269: David Mager. 270: Bill Stormont/The Stock Market. 272: David Mager.

Handbook: David Mager: pp R4, R5, R15

State Specific Credits: TX2: b. Roy Morsch/The Stock Market. TX3: t.l. John Lemker/Earth Scenes; b.r. Tom Bean; t.r. & b.l. Bob Daemmrich/The Image Works. TX4: b.l. Steve Elmore/The Stock Market; b.l. John D. Cunningham/Visuals Unlimited. TX8: b.r. & t.l. Jim Sugar Photography/ Corbis; t.r. Courtesy of Panhandle-Plains Historical Museum, Canyon, Texas. TX10: b. Texas DOT. TX11: c. Ross Frid/Visuals Unlimited. TX12: b.r. & t.l. Ross Frid/Visuals Unlimited. TX14: b. Superstock.

R32

REFERENCE--NOT TO BE
TAKEN FROM THIS ROOM

ROCHESTER COLLEGE
MUIRHEAD LIBRARY
800 WEST AVON ROAD
ROCHESTER HILLS MI 48307